# Early Childhood Staff Meeting Shiurim:
# The Collection

*49 Inspirations for a Jewish Discussion ~*

*Five years of professional development opportunities*

**Maxine Segal Handelman**
**United Synagogue of Conservative Judaism**
**Early Childhood Education Consultant**

Cover Art Molly-Rose Arnstein

Published by the United Synagogue of Conservative Judaism
Copyright © 2010 United Synagogue of Conservative Judaism
ISBN 978-0-615-39607-1

# Table of Contents

# Praise for Staff Meeting Shiurim

*Used the August Shiur to start our staff meeting with old and new staff talking at length about finding a teacher and finding a friend. It was a great way to start and truly impressed our new staff on the bonds and support of their colleagues. Best,*

- **Mindy Citera**
  Bet Torah Nursery School
  Mt. Kisco, NY

*What I love best about your approach in the shiurim is the fact that everyone can pull meaning from something in it. Even for staff of mine who aren't Jewish, I have had it expressed that the spiritual foundation of our program is meaningful to them. The shiurim hit people on a basic "gut" level and makes it a very simple tool to use as just that or as a springboard for more involved discussion.*

- **Denise Abadi**
  Charlotte Jewish Preschool
  Charlotte, NC

*I have been enjoying and benefiting from your Shiurim. They have become a regular part of our monthly staff meetings, and I truly believe the staff looks forward to them. In a way, they have brought us closer, and infused us with a greater sense of why we do what we do. So, thank you!*

- **Julie Oudin**
  Beth Yeshurun Day School
  Houston, TX

*As always, I enjoy your shiurim. I use them at the end of my staff's meetings so we can leave with some words of Judaism. Sometimes we don't have enough time and I found out that some teachers come prepared to the meetings with the Parsha and look forward to the shiur page!*

- **Silvia Kogan**
  Ilene M Rubin Nursery School
  East Meadow Jewish Center
  East Meadow, NY

*I used your Shiur twice at two different meetings and I loved using it! Todah Rabah!*

- **Judy Jacks Berman**
  Rose Family Early Childhood Education Center
  Congregation Beth Shalom
  Overland Park, KS

# Introduction

## Early Childhood Staff Meeting Shiurim Guides for Jewish Discussions

Judaism is about asking questions, engaging in dialogue, wrestling with text and ideas. In a Jewish early childhood program, each member of the staff is a Jewish educator. It is essential that early childhood Jewish educators engage in ongoing Jewish education, especially Torah l'shma --study for its own sake.

For five years, USCJ's department of education provided early childhood directors of USCJ Synagogue and Schechter early childhood programs with a Staff Meeting Shiur – a lesson consisting of text and questions, to be used to stimulate Jewish discussion during staff meetings. The text may come from such traditional sources as Torah or Midrash, it may be a contemporary quote, a poem or an excerpt from a story, or it may be something truly alternative that lends itself to a worthy discussion.

Points to consider:

- Each shiur (pronounced shee-or) should lead to a 20- to 25-minute discussion.

- The shiur requires little or no prerequisite knowledge.

- The shiur can be used any time during the month. If the text is part of the weekly Torah cycle it would come from a portion read in the second half of the month, and if it relates to a holiday the holiday, too, will fall in the second half of the month.

- There are very few "right" answers.

- You may not want to address every question.

- That said, the final question of each shiur addresses how the text and the discussion relate to practice in the early childhood program. Be sure to leave enough time to grapple with the last question.

- Have a TaNaK - Hebrew Bible - on hand to check texts surrounding or related to the given text.

Finally, we recommend giving serious consideration to inviting the synagogue or school rabbi to participate in (NOT lead) the shiur discussion. This is beneficial for many reasons:

- The rabbi is a source of Jewish information.

- The rabbi can help create a Jewish connection for staff members who have personal religious questions and may not have their own rabbi.

- The rabbi's involvement in the ongoing Jewish education of the EC staff gives the congregation or larger school community the message that the EC program is an important part of the synagogue or school.

- The rabbi and the teachers will have the opportunity to get to know each other informally. As a result, the EC staff may become more comfortable with the rabbi coming into the classroom for unstructured informal visits.

As the rabbi serves as the institution's mara d'atra, or religious authority, it may be helpful to have the rabbi take part in the discussion to help address any questions about religious practice in the early childhood program.

# Kicking the Year Off Right

## The Importance of Teachers and Early Childhood Education

*September 2005*

---

Those who uphold the community are like stars forever. Who are they? The ones who teach the young.

**- Baba Batra 8b**

What is learned in early childhood is absorbed in the blood.

**- Avot de Rabbi Natan 24**

---

**Questions for Discussion:**

1. The rabbis of the time of the Talmud held the potential of early childhood in high regard. Why might they have felt this way?

2. Rabbi Natan is quotes as saying that the lessons of early childhood are "absorbed in the blood?" Which of your own childhood experiences do you believe were absorbed in your blood?

3. The commandment to teach our children is found in the Torah, Deuteronomy 11:19: *And you shall teach them* [all of the commandments] *to your children, and you shall speak of them when you sit in your house, and when you walk on the way, and when you lie down, and when you rise up.* What do you as a Jewish educator need to know in order to fulfill this commandment?

4. As a Jewish early childhood teacher, you uphold your community. What does this mean? How would you like to see this recognized by the community?

5. According to the rabbis, the experiences children have in your classroom will leave lasting impressions and form the foundation of each child's Jewish identity. What, therefore, should be included in these experiences?

---

## Separation/New Attachments, Teachers and Friends

*August 2006*

---

יְהוֹשֻׁעַ בֶּן פְּרַחְיָה וְנִתַּאי הָאַרְבֵּלִי קִבְּלוּ מֵהֶם. יְהוֹשֻׁעַ בֶּן פְּרַחְיָה אוֹמֵר : עֲשֵׂה
לְךָ רַב, וּקְנֵה לְךָ חָבֵר, וֶהֱוֵי דָן אֶת כָּל הָאָדָם לְכַף זְכוּת

Joshua ben Perahiah and Nittai the Arbelite received [the oral tradition] from them [their teachers]. Joshua ben Perahiah says: provide a teacher for yourself; acquire a friend for yourself; and judge everyone favorably.

- **Pirke Avot 1:6**

---

### Questions for Discussion:

1. Diana Ganger says that the experience usually called "separation" is better viewed as "creating new attachments." As children come back to school, one of the first important things a teacher must do is help them and their families create these new attachments so they may have a successful year. What do the rabbis consider to be important attachments?

2. In an online article, Rabbi Fredi Cooper describes finding a friend and teacher in one classmate when she began rabbinical school. She writes, "What a blessing in life when the teacher and the friend reside in one individual . . . and what a blessing when this person comes into your life when you least expect it!!" (http://www.jrf.org/) In your life, when have you provided yourself with a teacher, or acquired for yourself a friend? Have you found both in one person? How has this been a blessing in your life?

3. In the Talmud, *Taanit 7a*, the rabbis teach that a friend serves three functions. The first is as a catalyst for increased success in Torah study, the second is in offering constructive criticism (and being offered constructive criticism in return), and the third is in providing good advice in all areas and acting as a discreet confidant who can be trusted with all life's secrets and challenges. What other functions would you assign to a friend? What functions would you assign to a teacher?

4. As we help children and families create new attachments and acquire new friends, how can this quote from Pirke Avot guide our intentions? How can you insure that you are a teacher whom each child and family would seek to provide for themselves? How do you help children make friends who will help them face life's challenges and achieve their potential?

---

## School's Vision/Excellence in Jewish Early Childhood Education

*August 2007*

---

אֲנִי וְאַתָּה נְשַׁנֶּה אֶת הָעוֹלָם.
אֲנִי וְאַתָּה אָז יָבוֹאוּ כְּבָר כֻּלָּם.

*A-ni V'-a-ta ne-sha-neh et ha-o lam,*
*A-ni V'-a-ta az ya-vo-u kvar ku-lam*

**- Arik Einstein and Miki Gabriellov, popular Israeli folk song**

The teachers love being early childhood teachers, but often the vision of the school is not clear to them. They are too often not full partners in the Jewish vision.

**-Michelle Rapchik-Levin, reflecting on her work with Jewish early childhood teachers at the CAJE Early Childhood pre-conference August 5, 2007**

---

**Questions for Discussion:**

1. As you prepare for the new school year, what do you know about your school's vision? Are you are a partner in your school's Jewish vision?

2. Dream a little - what would it take to change the world through the kind of experiences you create at your school? What kinds of people would you like your students and their families to be when they leave your school?

3. In Pirke Avot 2:21 (Ethics of the Fathers) we are told: *You are not required to complete the task, but neither are you free to desist from it.* What role do you play in your school's vision? How do you find out more? How do you go about taking an active part in making sure the vision, if it is a good vision, works as a guiding force in the school? If it's not a good vision, how do you go about changing it?

4. What are the key elements that make early childhood education Jewish?

5. What are the key elements that make Jewish early childhood education excellent?

6. Which of these elements already are a part of your classroom and school? How do you begin to adopt those elements that are not a part of your school culture and reality?

---

# Jewish Education and
# Other Jewish School Issues

## Working in a Jewish School/Families' Jewish Journeys

*February 2007*

---

"Your responsibility is much more than the child, it's to teach the family how to be a family, a Jewish family. That's your sacred responsibility."

**- Rabbi Ed Feinstein, senior rabbi at Valley Beth Shalom in Encino, CA, speaking to directors at the annual conference of the Early Childhood Educators of Reform Judaism, 2006.**

---

**Questions for Discussion:**

1. Midway through this school year, it is worthwhile to stop and reflect. What does it mean to work in a Jewish school? What does it mean to you?

2. What are the crucial elements of yourself that you bring to your teaching? How do your own beliefs inform your teaching? How much does your own practice reflect the life of the classroom? If there are large discrepancies, how do you reconcile them – or don't you?

3. How do we teach families to be Jewish families? How could we reach families in even stronger ways? Share a story of a family that you know increased its involvement in Jewish life because of the experience the child or family had in your school.

4. We read in the Talmud, "Education begins at the very moment of birth" (Sotah 47a). We know that early childhood education is the gateway to Jewish life. So how do we make sure that the Jewish life and experiences and education in our classrooms in which children are engaged are strong enough and enticing enough to draw families in and send them on their own Jewish journeys?

## Non-Jews in Jewish Schools, Part 1

*December 2007*

---

In North America today, at least 100,000 non-Jewish women are raising their children as Jews. These women deserve the support, encouragement, and gratitude of the organized Jewish community. A woman makes a great sacrifice and undertakes a great commitment when she raises a child in a religious tradition different from her own.

**- The Mother's Circle Program FAQ, http://www.themotherscircle.org/**

R. Samuel bar Naḥmani said in R. Jonathan's name: Whoever teaches Torah to the son of his neighbor it is as if he gave birth to him.

**- Sanhedrin 19b**

---

*(Note: this shiur is the first of two addressing the issues of non-Jews in Jewish schools. In February 2008 we will look at these quotes again, with more questions to ponder. Each of these shiurim will have only two questions, to encourage meatier discussions.)*

**Questions for Discussion:**

1. Many Jewish early childhood programs today are populated by two-Jewish parent families, intermarried families (with one Jewish parent) and non-Jewish families (with no Jewish parent). Additionally, many Jewish early childhood programs employ both Jewish and non-Jewish teachers, and although this is less common may be run by a non-Jewish director. The role of non-Jews in Jewish schools is a heavily debated topic. If your school fits this description in any way, discuss the benefits and challenges a mixed population presents to a Jewish school.

2. Have you ever wondered how to handle the circle-time conversation when a child wants to talk about his Christmas tree? Ever listened to a group of children discuss who "is Hanukah" and who "is Christmas" and been unsure of whether to jump in and what to say? Ever felt embarrassed because you weren't able to pronounce the words of the blessing you're supposed to say before snack? Ever felt really proud of yourself for learning which blessing goes with which food, but then had no answer for the parent who asks you why we light two candles for Shabbat? What does it feel like to teach in a Jewish school with lots of non-Jewish kids? What does it feel like not to be Jewish and to teach in a Jewish school? What makes it a positive situation? What could make it feel better?

---

## Too Jewish/Non Jewish Families, Part 2

*February 2008*

---

In North America today, at least 100,000 non-Jewish women are raising their children as Jews. These women deserve the support, encouragement, and gratitude of the organized Jewish community. A woman makes a great sacrifice and undertakes a great commitment when she raises a child in a religious tradition different from her own.

**- The Mother's Circle Program FAQ, http://www.themotherscircle.org/**

R. Samuel bar Naḥmani said in R. Jonathan's name: Whoever teaches Torah to the son of his neighbor it is as if he gave birth to him.

**- Sanhedrin 19b**

---

*(Note: this shiur of the second of two addressing the issues of non-Jews in Jewish schools. We began the discussion in December 2007. Following are more questions to ponder. Each of these shiurim have only two questions, to encourage meatier discussions.)*

**Questions for Discussion:**

1. Almost every Jewish early childhood school grapples with the "too Jewish" issue – parents from across the spectrum who question why a school does certain things, sometimes complaining (or implying) that the school is "too Jewish." Mindy Citera, a director in New York, says parents can "use it or lose it." She explains, "We provide our Jewish curriculum intertwined in our developmentally appropriate secular curriculum and Jewish families and non-Jewish families use what applies to their families and 'lose' the content that is not." Whatever the stance, each director and staff member must be intentional about creating a school culture that helps parents understand, appreciate and buy into the Jewish curriculum, beginning with the initial tour or interview. How is this buy-in created in your school? How do you and the rest of the staff respond to parents when they complain that the school is too Jewish?

2. According to the second quote above, the rabbis of the Talmud say that we as teachers are like parents when we give children a Jewish education. How can each one of us make this Jewish experience most authentic, when we teachers come from all kinds of backgrounds, ranging from Jewish scholars to Jewish with limited Jewish knowledge to not Jewish? Assuming that all parents have enrolled their children in the school with complete buy-in to the Jewish curriculum, how do we most appropriately and fully involve and include every child in the Jewish experience of the school, knowing that the school experience may be somewhat to very disparate from the children's home experiences?

---

## Connecting with Day Schools – Continuing Children's Jewish Education Journey

*August 2008*

> Cut off from a living and vital Jewish community, Jewish education is meaningless talk with little connection to values, culture, or purpose. Great synagogues must be a central component in any effort to fill our day schools as part of a general revitalization of Jewish life.
>
> **- Barry Shrage, "Jewish Renaissance: A Broad Vision for the Next Decade," in 10 Years of Believing in Jewish Day School Education, Partnership for Excellence in Jewish Education (PEJE), 2007**

**Questions for Discussion:**

1. How does the Jewish education you provide to your children and families create a connection with the community? How else could it?

2. What path has your own Jewish education taken? What would you like to learn more about? Where could you go to make this happen?

3. *Teach a child in the way he should go, and he will not stray from it even when he gets older* (Proverbs 22:6). While this sentiment from Proverbs is lovely, sometimes the investment you have made in your students' Jewish education needs some protection if it is to grow instead of withering away. What do you envision as ideal paths for your children (and their families)? What do you know about the options available in your community for Jewish education once your children leave the early childhood program? How can you start to pave these paths now?

4. At the PEJE conference in April 2008, day school leaders struggled with how best to connect with Jewish early childhood programs. They heard the message that it's not ok just to send the admissions director in to "get the list," but that they must form real, mutually supportive relationships, beginning with the head of school and the early childhood director. Before you recommend the synagogue's religious school or any local day schools to your children's parents, what do you want from a relationship with those schools? What do you need to know about those programs? What resources can they provide for your school? What can your school do for them?

You can read the entire article quoted above at:
http://peje.org/publications/books_and_articles/200710_PEJE_10Yr_Report.pdf, pp.9-14.

## Jewish Environment

*August 2009*

---

Rabban Johanan ben Zakkai had five disciples, and these (included):…Rabbi Joshua ben Hananiah. He used to recount their praise:…Rabbi Joshua ben Hananiah – happy is she who gave birth to him.

**- Pirke Avot, excerpts, Chapter 2, Mishnaim 10 & 11**

When Rabbi Joshua ben Hananiah was an infant, his mother used to carry him in his cradle to the beit midrash (house of study), so his ears would become accustomed to the sounds of the Torah.

**- Jerusalem Talmud Yebamot 1, 6**

---

**Questions for Discussion:**

1. How does your school help accustom the ears of your children to the sounds of Torah – in other words, to the sights, sounds and rhythms of Jewish life?

2. How did your parents help foster your education? If you are a parent, how do you help facilitate your child's education?

3. Why was Rabbi Joshua ben Hananiah praised on the account of his mother? What were her goals for her son? What did she do to achieve her dreams?

4. What are the goals of the parents who bring their children to your school? How do you know? Do you meet these goals?

The environment is a child's third teacher, in conjunction with the teacher and the parents. A Jewish identity is built not only on Shabbat songs sung at circle time on Fridays, but also on the smell of challah in the school halls, Shabbat books for a child to look at by him or herself, and candlesticks a child can pretend with in the dramatic play area. We must create the Jewish environment in our schools with much intentionality. The Vision for Conservative Early Childhood Programs suggests many ways to build and enhance the Jewish environment. Look at the list and see which ideas you can implement into your school this year: http://uscj.org/images/ECE_vision.pdf (or look under the Education tab at http://www.uscj.org).

---

# Fall Holidays (Elul and Tishre)

## Shofar Blowing in Elul

*September 2006*

---

> It is the custom to sound the shofar daily after the morning service during the month of Elul, beginning the second day of Rosh Chodesh (the first day of Elul). We blow Tekiah, Shevarim, and Teruah. We do not blow the shofar the day before Rosh Hashanah to make a distinction between the voluntary blowing during Elul and the mandatory sounding on Rosh Hashanah. The reason the shofar is sounded during Elul is to move people to repentance.
>
> **– Code of Jewish Law (Kitzur Shulchan Arukh), Rabbi Solomon Ganzfried**

---

**Questions for Discussion:**

1. Rosh Chodesh Elul – the days marking the new moon and thus the new month -- are August 24 and 25 this year. The 24th actually is the last day of the Hebrew month of Av, and the 25th is the first day of the Hebrew month of Elul. So August 25 is the second day of Rosh Chodesh, but the first day of Elul, and this is the day we begin to blow the shofar every morning except Shabbat. That continues until 2 days before Rosh Hashanah, so September 21 is the last of these "voluntary" shofar blowings. You can hear the shofar sounds (Tekiah, Shevarim, and Teruah) at http://www.torahtots.com/holidays/rosh/roshstr.htm. Who on your staff can blow shofar? How many different shofrot (plural of shofar) can you collect for the children to see over the next month?

2. What different experiences have you had as you've listened to the shofar? What does the shofar make you think about? What does it make you feel?

3. *The Code of Jewish Law* says that the shofar is sounded during this month to move people to repentance. The Jewish New Year, Rosh Hashanah, is a time of reflection and repentance, a time we seek to improve ourselves. Do we really need a month to wake up to this task of self-reflection and repentance? How can hearing the shofar help achieve this?

4. It is likely that your school will begin with all or a great part of the month of Elul remaining. How do you think the children will react to hearing the shofar blown each morning at school? How might it help your children wake up during this time before Rosh Hashanah? How can you involve the families in this shofar blowing?

---

## High Holiday Greetings/Sayver Panim Yafot

*September 2008*

**Questions for Discussion:**

1. A new year has just begun in school, and a new Jewish year is quickly approaching. What are your hopes and dreams for this new year?

2. For Rosh Hashanah, the Jewish New Year, there are specific greetings which we offer to people. In the weeks before Rosh Hashanah, we say "L'Shanah Tovah Tikatevu," which literally means, "May you be written [in the Book of Life] for a good year." We might also say "Shanah Tovah" (A good year), "Shanah tovah u'mitukah" (A good sweet year), or simply, "Gut yohr" (Yiddish, Good year). Between Rosh Hashanah and Yom Kippur, the tone changes a little. We say "G'mar Chatimah Tovah" which literally means "May you finally be sealed [in the Book of Life] for good." We also say "Tzom kal" (An easy fast). On Yom Kippur, we say "L'shanah tovah tikatayvu v'te-cha-taymu" (May you be inscribed and sealed [in the Book of Life] for a good year). What do all these greetings tell us about the Jewish hopes and dreams for the new year? What is the Book of Life? (to answer this question, check out a study guide at http://www.uscj.org/Koach/documents/bookoflife.doc)

**Inside:** Wishing you a happy, healthy and prosperous New Year!

http://jewishfunnybone.com

3. In Judaism, we have the value of Sayver Panim Yafot, essentially, having a pleasant demeanor. How does it affect a moment when we begin an interaction with someone with a sayver panim yafot? Role play an encounter two ways – once with a sayver panim yafot, and once with a grouchy attitude. How do each of these moments feel? How might a habit of sayver panim yafot and the High Holiday greetings set a strong, positive tone for the entire year?

4. What role will the High Holiday greetings play in your classroom? How will you instill in your children a habit of sayver panim yafot? Does this work even with infants?

## Tashlich

*September 2009*

---

When he gets to the pier, Rabbi Neil is saying, "Tashlich is the time we apologize for things we wish we hadn't done. Tashlich means to throw. We throw away things we don't like or don't need. Tashlich is like cleaning your heart's closet. A new year, a clean heart."

Just this summer, Izzy and Miriam cleaned their toy closet and gave a lot away. Now it seems bigger. Sometimes he just opens the closet to see how clean it is.

**- *New Year at the Pier* by April Halprin Wayland, Dial Books for Young Readers, 2009\*.**

---

**Questions for Discussion:**

1. What do you know about the tradition of tashlich, the ritual that we perform on Rosh Hashanah? As a group, share what all of you know to get a full picture. Traditionally, tashlich is observed on the first day of Rosh Hashanah, but this year it will be observed on Sunday, September 20, the second day of Rosh Hashanah, since the first day of Rosh Hashanah is Shabbat. You can find a good explanation of tashlich at http://www.uscj.org/TashlikhCasting_Sins5674.html.

2. Where's the most interesting place you've ever done tashlich? If you've never done Tashlich, what living body of water would you chose?

3. There are no set blessings that are part of tashlich ceremony, only some suggested psalms and readings, such as this excerpt from Psalm 130:

   *Out of the depths I call to You; Lord, hear my cry, heed my plea. Be attentive to my prayers, to my sigh of supplication. Who could endure, Lord, if You kept count of every sin? But forgiveness is Yours, therefore we revere You.*

   The prayers in synagogue on Rosh Hashanah are in a communal language: "Inscribe **us** in the Book of Life," and "Forgive and pardon all **our** sins." But tashlich is a very personal time to think about your own mistakes, just between you, God, and the fish. Do psalms like this one, and the other readings at the United Synagogue webpage listed above, help you do the self-reflecting that Rosh Hashanah is all about? What works best for you?

4. How can you rewrite this excerpt from psalms to create something appropriate for young children to say when they do tashlich? What would work for two-year-olds? For fours? What does *teshuvah* (repentance) look like for young children, anyway?

\* There hasn't been a book about tashlich since *The Rosh Hashanah Walk*. *New Year at the Pier* is a very good story about a kid's experience with tashlich and making amends with people. Really good for 4s and 5s, maybe even 3s.

---

## Ushpizin/Sukkah Guests

*September 2007*

> When you sit in the sukkah, "the shade of faithfulness," the Shechina spreads Her wings over you and... Abraham, five other righteous ones, and King David make their dwelling with you.... Thus you should rejoice with a shining countenance each and every day of the festival together with these guests who lodge with you.
>
> **- Zohar Emor, 103b**

### Questions for Discussion:

1. What do guests add to our celebration of Sukkot and our time in the sukkah?

2. If you build a sukkah at your house, tell your favorite story about a guest who shared a meal with you there. If you've dined in someone else's sukkah, relate your favorite sukkah visit (and be sure to share the reasons why it was the best). If you have no personal sukkah experience, go to http://www.youtube.com, search "sukkah" and "Sukkot" and watch a couple of videos. My personal favorites include "Sukkah Preparations – Sukkah Building," "The Sukkot Shake," "Sukkot" and "happy sukkot."

3. Each night of Sukkot, a prayer is recited asking a biblical figure to come and visit in the sukkah. The seven *ushpizin* –guests – are usually Abraham, Isaac, Jacob, Moses, Aaron, Joseph, and David. Various traditions, both medieval and modern, invite female guests, or *ushpizot*, to the sukkah as well. According to the tradition of medieval Italian kabbalist Menachem Azariah of Fano, the ushpizot are Sarah, Miriam, Deborah, Hannah, Abigail, Huldah, and Esther, because these women are distinguished in the Talmud as prophetesses. Other traditions include such biblical figures as Rebecca, Leah, Rachel, Dinah, Tamar, or Ruth.

    What do you know about any of these people? Why would our tradition include inviting "imaginary" guests to the sukkah?

4. Having ushpizin in the sukkah along with real guests, family and friends, gives children an opportunity to practice the mitzvah of *hachnasat orchim*. How might you use the concept of ushpizin and the stories of these biblical characters to increase the joy and meaning of your class's Sukkot celebration this year?

Lev Midrash/Simchat Torah

*October 2005*

# TORAH LEV

## OUR LAND ... OUR HEART ... OUR BEGINNING

The last word of the Torah is Yisrael – Israel – ישראל

The first word is B'raisheet– בראשית

the last letter of the last word (Yisrael) ל

and first letter of the first word (B'raisheet) ב

form the word – Lev לב which means Heart

©DLD

**Questions for Discussion:**

1. On Simchat Torah we finish reading the Torah and immediately begin again. Why do we do this, year after year?

2. How does Torah touch your heart?

3. Represented by a piece of jewelry in the illustration above, (because we can express ourselves in many different ways), this sentiment, created by the seamless act of ending and beginning again, has been explained in many ways. One commentator tells us that the Torah is the lev – the heart – of the Jewish people. Arnold Gluck wrote in Torat Hayim – Living Torah in October 2, 1999: "In that magical and sacred moment of renewal, the last letter of the Torah, lamed, joins the first letter of the Torah, bet, to spell out the Hebrew word lev, which means heart. Like a wedding ring that has no beginning and no end, the linkage of the lamed and the bet that forms the word lev reminds us that the Torah links our hearts to the Heart of the universe. The Torah was given to us to incline our hearts toward God and toward one another." In what other ways might you explain the lev we discover on Simchat Torah?

4. How can you insure that your children discover and embrace the lev of Torah in your classroom?

Some material from:
http://urj.org/Articles/index.cfm?id=3122&pge_prg_id=14422&pge_id=3724

## Shmini Atzeret

*October 2008*

אֱ-לֹהֵינוּ וֵא-לֹהֵי אֲבוֹתֵינוּ,
זְכוֹר אָב נִמְשַׁךְ אַחֲרֶיךָ כַּמַּיִם, בֵּרַכְתּוֹ כְּעֵץ שָׁתוּל עַל פַּלְגֵי
מַיִם, גְּנַנְתּוֹ הִצַּלְתּוֹ מֵאֵשׁ וּמִמַּיִם, דְּרַשְׁתּוֹ בְּזָרְעוֹ עַל כָּל מָיִם.
הקהל עונה: בַּעֲבוּרוֹ אַל תִּמְנַע מָיִם.
זְכוֹר הַנּוֹלָד בִּבְשׂוֹרַת יֻקַּח נָא מְעַט מַיִם, וְשַׂחְתָּ לְהוֹרוֹ
לְשָׁחֲטוֹ לִשְׁפֹּךְ דָּמוֹ כַּמַּיִם זָהֵר גַּם הוּא לִשְׁפֹּךְ לֵב כַּמַּיִם,
חָפַר וּמָצָא בְּאֵרוֹת מָיִם.
הקהל עונה: בְּצִדְקוֹ חֹן חַשְׁרַת מָיִם.
זְכוֹר טָעַן מַקְלוֹ וְעָבַר יַרְדֵּן מַיִם, יִחַד לֵב וְגָל אֶבֶן מִפִּי בְאֵר
מַיִם, כְּנֶאֱבַק לוֹ שַׂר בָּלוּל מֵאֵשׁ וּמִמַּיִם, לָכֵן הִבְטַחְתּוֹ הֱיוֹת
עִמּוֹ בָּאֵשׁ וּבַמָּיִם.
הקהל עונה: בַּעֲבוּרוֹ אַל תִּמְנַע מָיִם.
**שָׁאַתָּה הוּא ה׳ אֱ-לֹהֵינוּ, מַשִּׁיב הָרוּחַ וּמוֹרִיד הַגָּשֶׁם**

"Our God and the God of our forefathers:
Remember the Patriarch [Abraham], who was drawn behind
You like water. You blessed him like a tree replanted alongside
streams of water. You shielded him, You rescued him from fire and
from water. You tested him when he sowed upon all waters.
*Cong. – For his sake, do not hold water back!*

Remember the one [Isaac] born with the tidings of, 'Let some
water be brought.' You told his father to slaughter him – to
spill his blood like, water. He too was scrupulous to pour his
heart like water. He dug and discovered wells of water.
*Cong. – For the sake of his righteousness, grant abundant water!*

Remember the one [Jacob] who carried his staff
and crossed the Jordan's water.
He dedicated his heart and rolled a stone
off the mouth of a well of water,
as when he was wrestled by an angel composed of fire and water.
Therefore You pledged to remain with him through fire and water.
*Cong. – For his sake, do not hold water back!*

Chazzan: *For You are Adonai our God,
Who makes the wind blog and makes the rain descend.*

- **Excerpt, *Tefilat HaGeshem* (Prayer for Rain) recited on Sh'mini Atzeret**

## Questions for Discussion:

1.  Sh'mini Atzeret is a little-known holiday that comes at the end of Sukkot, the day before Simchat Torah, on the 22nd of Tishre. The name literally means "the eighth day assembly," although it is not technically part of Sukkot. The holiday is derived from the regulations in Lev. 23:36. Rabbinic literature explains this as the day when God invited us to remain together with God for one additional day. What do you think of this idea of extending the party for just one more day?

2.  On Sh'mini Atzeret, we say the prayer for rain, which is excerpted above, and then add the final line to our daily prayer - *Mashiv haruach u'morid hagashem* (You cause the wind to blow and the rain to fall) - that we continue to say until Passover. Jews all over the world add this prayer, even though it might not be the proper season for rain where they live. Why might that be? What season is it in Israel? What might this prayer cycle have meant for people making the pilgrimage to Jerusalem for Sukkot, and going back again for Passover?

3.  In the prayer above, God is asked to provide rain on the merit of our forefathers – Abraham, Isaac, and Jacob. Who else in the Torah has connections to water? Be sure to try and think about Biblical women too. How are you connected to water?

4.  How are the lessons of Sh'mini Atzeret relevant to your early childhood classroom? What do children know about rain? How do they interact with rain? How does an understanding of Sh'mini Atzeret help you to frame the rain in a Jewish context?

# Hanukkah

## December Dilemma

*December 2005*

---

It happened the same way every winter, when the world grew cold and afternoons became dark long before dinnertime....

One morning, Emma's father raised the shades in her room and said, "Sweetheart! Tonight's the first night of Hanukkah! Time to get out the menorah!"

_____

Then one day, Emma's mother pulled down boxes of Christmas ornaments from the top shelf of the closet. "Well, Pumpkin, shall we pick out the Christmas tree this morning?" she asked.

_____

After the holidays, Emma helped wrap the Hanukkah menorah and the Christmas ornaments and put them away for next year. But she remembered the bright winter lights in the dark winter nights for a long, long time.

**- Excerpts from *Light the Lights! A Story about Celebrating Hanukkah and Christmas* by Margaret Moorman, Scholastic, Cartwheel Books, NY: 1994.**

---

*More and more, our preschool children bring varied experiences to school with them. Every winter we grapple with the "December dilemma," when Christmas and Hanukkah go head to head in our schools. We must remember that children living in the general American culture, and especially children from interfaith families, will be exposed to diverse religious lifecycle practices. We must strive to create an atmosphere that provides acceptance, respect and value for diversity. Our sensitive support and reinforcement of both our children's experiences and our school's mission will best offer the opportunity for children to feel connected both to the communities of which their family are a part and their school communities.*

**Questions for Discussion:**

1. How typical is Emma's experience among the children you teach?

2. How familiar is this experience to you personally, among your family and friends?

3. How comfortable are you with this family's practice?

4. We strive to validate every child in our program. How do you respond when a child wants to talk about her family's Christmas tree?

5. Hanukkah is the celebration of the Maccabbees' successful struggle to redeem our right to live a fully observant Jewish life. Given your school's population, how can you teach Hanukkah, with its true message of taking advantage of our hard-won freedom to live as Jews?

---

## Resources:

- Albee, Sarah. *Celebrate with Blue! A Book of Winter Holidays*, Simon Spotlight/Nickelodeon, 2005. (board book)

- Axford, Elizabeth. *Merry Christmas Happy Hanukkah: A Multilingual Songbook and CD*, Piano Press, 1999.

- Gertz, Susan Enid. *Hanukkah and Christmas at My House*, Willow and Laurel Press, 1992.

- Older, Effin. *My Two Grandmothers*, Harcourt Children's Books, 2000.

- Santomero, Angela. *A Blue's Clues Holiday*, Simon Spotlight/Nickelodeon, 2004

- Zeskind, Margie and Sheila Silverberg. *The S.A.G.A. Approach (Sensitive Alternatives for Guiding Affectively)*, SheMar Productions, Inc. 1996.

## Articles to Share:

- The December Dilemma by Ron Wolfson, http://hillel.myjewishlearning.com/holidays/Hanukkah/TO_Hanukkah_Themes/W olfson_December_864.htm *(especially good for a Jewish family considering borrowing some Christmas traditions)*

- Holiday Guidelines for Interfaith Families by Julie Andrews Horowitz, http://hillel.myjewishlearning.com/holidays/Hanukkah/TO_Hanukkah_Themes/W olfson_December_864/Interfaith_Holidays.htm

## Hanukkah Candle Debate

*December 2006*

---

Beit Shammai rules: On the first day of Hanukkah, we light eight candles; each day thereafter, we diminish the lights by one. Beit Hillel rules: On the first day of Hanukkah, we light one candle; each day thereafter, we increase the lights by one.

Rabbi Yossi bar Abin and Rabbi Yossi bar Zvida differed on the motivations behind these rulings. One said Beit Shammai decided their rules according to the days that are yet to come; and Beit Hillel decided their rules according to the days that have passed.

The other said Beit Shammai decided their rule according to the decreasing number of sacrifices offered at the Temple each day of Sukkot (Sukkot is the biblical model for the post-biblical holiday of Hanukkah) and Beit Hillel decided their rule according to the dictum: one increases things of holiness, and does not decrease them.

**- Shabbat 21a**

---

**Questions for Discussion:**

1. The Talmud records both sides of this *makhloket* (debate) over how many candles we light each night of Hanukkah. Whose ruling, Beit Shammai (the house or disciples of Rabbi Shammai) or Beit Hillel, do we follow today?

2. Hillel bases his opinion on the principle that "on matters of holiness, we should only increase." How is this statement relevant to your life? How can we increase the level of holiness in our lives?

3. In this text, two rabbis, Rabbi Yossi bar Abin and Rabbi Yossi bar Zvida, offer their opinion on the motivations behind these rulings. Here are two modern opinions:

   Rabbi Nina Beth Cardin wrote in Sh'ma magazine: "This choice of counting up or down encapsulates two approaches to life: Are the blessings of life so finite – so that with each one bestowed our cup is diminished? Or are they as infinite as the Source from which they come? And even if they are finite; do we imagine a growing darkness as each is used up, or do we gather all the revealed ones together, basking in the light that grows with each new blessing? How we answer these questions colors the way we receive each new day and each new blessing."

   Shprintzee Herskovits wrote in the on-line Torah shiur from Midreshet Harova – Advanced Torah Academy for Women: "Hillel and Shammai saw the lighting of Hanukkah candles as representing how we feel about the holiday of Hanukkah. Both agreed that we should experience increased excitement as Hanukkah goes on. However Shammai said that in reality, most people do not feel increased excitement as Hanukkah goes on. A person's excitement diminishes as he becomes accustomed to something. Hanukkah is no different; a person's excitement diminishes each day as he gets more

---

and more used to it. Therefore, Shammai said that our lighting candles should reflect the reality of how we feel and so we should light eight candles on the first day of Hanukkah (when our excitement is at its peak) and then gradually decrease the number to reflect our diminishing excitement. On the other hand Hillel said that we should light candles according to how we are SUPPOSED to feel. Given that our excitement is supposed to increase as Hanukkah goes on, we should start out lighting one candle and then increase the number until we get to eight – the peak of our excitement."
(http://www.midreshetharova.org.il/torah/view.asp?id=842)

In what other ways might you explain the motivations behind Hillel and Shammai's opposing rulings?

4. Jewish holidays span sundown to sundown; in other words, they begin the evening before the day of the holiday. In the early childhood program, we are faced with our own makhloket or debate about to Hanukkah candles. In our classrooms, do we light Hanukkah candles according to what day it actually is, or do we light the number of candles the children should expect to light that night at home? Either position may be supported: the first as it follows halakhah (Jewish law), the other, l'shem hinuch (for the sake of education), prepares the children for their family Hanukkah celebration that night. Either way, be sure to engage in this makhloket as a staff and agree on a unified custom for your school that every teacher can explain to parents.

## Hanukkah, Miracles and Being a Normal Mystic

*December 2008*

---

"Dear God, How come you did all those miracles in the old days and don't do any now?"

**- From *Children's Letters to God: The New Collection* compiled by Stuart Hample and Eric Marshall, NY: Workman Publishing, 1991.**

Miracle: 1: an extraordinary event manifesting divine intervention in human affairs 2: an extremely outstanding or unusual event, thing, or accomplishment

**– Merriam-Webster Dictionary**

---

**Questions for Discussion:**

1. Hanukkah is the holiday of miracles. What is/are the Hanukkah miracle(s)*?

2. Think about a moment that felt miraculous to you, and tell your colleagues about it. (Only one person gets to say "the birth of my child.") Describe your feelings at the time of the "miracle" and its lingering effects.

3. The battle commemorated on Hanukkah occurred between 168 and 165 BCE. We learn the history of Hanukkah from I Maccabees and II Maccabees, written around 135 BCE and 120 BCE respectively, which are found in the Apocrypha. (The Apocrypha are writings excluded from the Tanach – the Hebrew Bible.) We read:

   *"Maccabee with his men, led by the Lord, recovered the temple and city of Jerusalem.... The sanctuary was purified on the twenty-fifth of Kislev, the same day of the same month as that on which foreigners had profaned it. The Jews celebrated joyfully for eight days as on the Feast of Booths [Sukkot]. By public edict and decree they prescribed that the whole Jewish nation should celebrate these days every year."* (II Maccabees, 10: 1, 5-6, 8)

   The rabbis, writing the Talmud some 500 years later, bring up an entirely different miracle:

   *"What is the reason for Hanukkah? Our rabbis taught ... that when the Greeks entered the temple, they defiled all the oil there. When the Hasmoneans [Maccabees] beat the Greeks, only one cruse of oil that still bore the seal of the high priest could be found. Though it contained only enough oil for one day's lighting, a miracle occurred, and the lamp burned for eight days. The next year they ordained these days a holiday with songs and praises."* (Babylonian Talmud, *Shabbat* 21b)

   What can you make of these differing stories? Why would the rabbis stress the miracle of oil over the military victory? Why is the oil story still so popular?

---

4.  As a staff, do a little more research. Check out books like *Jewish Every Day* (Maxine Handelman, A.R.E. Publishing) and on-line resources like this study guide from Koach: http://www.uscj.org/Koach/documents/Hanukkah-04.pdf. When all of you feel like you have a good handle on the whole story of Hanukkah, develop a consistent version of the story to use throughout your school. Which miracles will you include? Discuss how the study and celebration of Hanukkah will spiral through the years at your school, increasing in complexity each year and building on the previous year's understandings.

For more information, see the article by Maxine Handelman at http://www.morim.org called "It's a Miracle!"

* The Hanukkah miracles include the vile of oil, enough for one day, lasting for eight days, and the victory of the tiny Maccabee army over the great Greek/Syrian army.

# Tu B'Shevat

## Caring for Trees

*January 2007*

> I am the Lorax. I speak for the trees.
> I speak for the trees, for the trees have no tongues.
>
> **- Dr. Seuss, *The Lorax***

**Questions for Discussion:**

1. How do we speak for trees? What do trees need said for them?

2. Have you ever tried to grow a tree? Did you grow it from seed or from a sapling? What happened in the end? Were you able to taste its fruit? Does it still grace your yard?

3. The Torah speaks for trees. For example, in Deuteronomy 20:19 it says:

   *When you shall besiege a city … you must not destroy its trees, wielding the ax against them. You may eat of them, but you must not cut them down. For is the tree of the field human, that it should be besieged by you?*

   And in Micah 4:4, the image of ultimate peace is:

   *But they shall sit every man under his vine and under his fig-tree; and none shall make them afraid.*

   What is our responsibility to trees, even when we are not making war on a city? What do we gain from a relationship with trees? Why are trees so important that they merit their own holiday – Tu B'Shevat, which falls on February 3 this year?

4. How do we communicate to our children the real responsibility they have to care for trees, and also for their world? What concrete experiences can we facilitate for children to help them accept this responsibility? Can planting seeds in class be done with enough respect (and persistence) to cultivate grown plants and saplings? What about adopting a tree on the school grounds to care for? Or the class purchasing trees in Israel? There are many Jewish tree stories at http://www.yourpage.org and information about trees and forests in Israel at http://www.jnf.org.

## Trees/Caring for the Earth

*January 2008*

---

"True, the trees went to a noble cause," Solomon concluded. "Yet, it's also true that because of me the forest is gone; therefore, it is upon me to bring it back."

**- From *Solomon and the Trees* by Matt Biers-Ariel, UAHC Press, 2001**

---

**Questions for Discussion:**

1. Think about a time when you planted a tree, helped clear away debris from a play area, created a bird sanctuary, or had a similar experience, and tell your colleagues about it. Describe your feelings upon approaching the task and upon finishing the job.

2. In recent years, and in recent months, areas of our country, including Southern California, have suffered great fires, which have affected trees and other wildlife. Yet a strange thing often happens after a fire. Trees begin to regenerate. In Southern California, some kinds of chaparral (a general term that applies to various types of brushland) have leaves that are coated with flammable resins, seeds that require intense heat for germination, and roots that are specially adapted to enable the plant to grow in areas that were recently burned. Furthermore, when the chaparral is burned many of the nutrients that have been locked up in it are released and recycled back into the soil. The Douglas fir, found in areas of the northwest, regenerates readily on sites that have been prepared by fire. In fact, nearly all the natural Douglas fir stands in the United States grew on ground that had burned. Common trees and shrubs often are able to sprout from surviving plant parts after a fire. This is a very hopeful response to tragedy. What lessons can we learn from the trees?

3. Rabbi Elazar ben Azaria, a Talmudic sage of the first century CE, said: "Any time our wisdom exceeds our good deeds, to what are we likened? To a tree whose branches are numerous but whose roots are few; then the wind comes and uproots it and turns it upside down. ...But when our good deeds exceed our wisdom, to what are we likened? To a tree whose branches are few but whose roots are numerous; even if all the winds of the world were to come and blow against it, they could not budge it from its place..." What are some actions young children can take to make positive changes in their world? How can young children become part of the regeneration process? In *Solomon and the Trees,* the forest is cut down to build the Temple in Jerusalem. Solomon makes sure that he is not only part of the problem but also part of the solution by planting new trees to regenerate the forest. Where are areas of your community that could benefit by becoming greener? How can your children be part of this process?

---

## Trees, Torah, Tu B'Shevat

*February 2006*

> עֵץ-חַיִּים הִיא לַמַּחֲזִיקִים בָּהּ וְתֹמְכֶיהָ מְאֻשָּׁר
> דְּרָכֶיהָ דַרְכֵי-נֹעַם וְכָל-נְתִיבוֹתֶיהָ שָׁלוֹם
>
> It is a Tree of Life to those who hold fast to it, and whoever holds onto it is happy. Her ways are ways of pleasantness and all its paths are peace.
>
> **- Proverbs 3:18, 3:17, from the liturgy for returning the Torah to the Holy Ark**

**Questions for Discussion:**

1. Jewish texts such as the one above refer to the Jewish people's holiest book, the Torah, as a tree – and not just any tree, but the Tree of Life, Aitz Hayim. What is it about a tree that might make it suitable for this analogy?

2. What's your favorite memory of a tree?

3. The Torah and the Jewish people are also compared to many of the seven species of fruits and grains that we eat to celebrate Tu B'Shevat, the New Year of the Trees. For example:

   - *If there is no flour, there is no Torah; if there is no Torah, there is no flour* (Pirke Avot 3:17).

   - *Why is the Torah compared to a fig tree? Because the fruit of most trees...is gathered all at once, but the fig's fruit is gathered gradually, little by little. And so the Torah. One studies a little each day and eventually learns much, because the Torah is not to be learned in one or even two years* (Midrash Numbers Rabbah 21:15).

   - *As no part of the date palm is wasted – its dates being eaten, its branches used for Hallel, its fronds for covering a Sukkah, its fibers for ropes, its leaves for sweeping, its planed trunk for the ceiling of houses – so are there no Jews without worth: some are versed in Bible, others know Mishnah, some in Talmud, others in Aggadah, some in deeds of piety and still others in deeds of charity* (Midrash Numbers Rabbah 3:1).

   What can these quotes (and others that you might know) tell us about the role of the Torah in our lives today? About our relationship with nature and the earth? About our relationships with each other?

4. What do you want to make sure your children know about trees? How will you weave the Torah through your celebration of Tu B'Shevat this year?

# Spring Holidays

## Purim Important Themes
*March 2006*

---

**PURIM MYSTERY**

Left, right, up, down, diagonal, and backwards. Where are these Purim words?

```
O V A S H T I T S A V A B
A H C E D R O M R U P M A
D M G A L L O W S R U E Q
D A N Q U E T H R E R G U
E T M H A V A M A H I I S
S A O S E H A A A T M L I
O N R O E S H S U S A L M
N O D R B A N Q U E T A E
A S E I R H H A D U E S G
M L C E O C I S H L O A I
H E H V S A A D A R L S L
C Y A H A M A N I A S H L
A Y I S H S A E P P P E A
O O Y A P U V R I U M K H
L N B H A H M A N A R E R
H I U C S C Q H I M M L A
S M I A T A A N I S L O M
I V H A M A N T A S H E N
M C N A H S U H S B E Y O
A G R O G G E R V A S H T
```

| | | |
|---|---|---|
| Achashveirosh | Hamantashen | Shekel |
| Adar | Matanos Levyonim | Shushan |
| Banquet | Megillah | Taanis |
| Esther | Mishloach Manos | Vashti |
| Gallows | Mordechai | |
| Grogger | Purim | |
| Haman | Seudah | |

- **From** http://www.shemayisrael.co.il/purim/mystery.htm

**Questions for Discussion:**

1. Purim is a time of stories, games, and frivolity. As a group, retell the Purim story. See if you can use all of the above words.

2. Which of the above words do you not recognize? Who can help you define all the terms? Can you be brave like Esther and ask for help when you need it?

3. While we play lots of games and engage in many silly behaviors, like dressing up, on Purim, we should not forget that behind all the hilarity, Purim has some serious messages. Look at the following text from Megillat Esther, the Book of Esther, which tells the story of Purim:

   *When Mordecai hears of Haman's plan to destroy the Jews, he sends word to Esther, charging her to go to the king and plead for the life of her people. She wavers, and he sends her this message:* "Do not imagine that you, of all the Jews, will escape with your life by being in the king's palace. On the contrary, if you keep silent in this crisis, relief and deliverance will come to the Jews from another quarter, while you and your father's house will perish. And who knows, perhaps you have attained to royal position for just such a crisis" (Esther 4:13-14).

   What are some of the themes of Purim that we learn from the above passage and others that you know?

4. Purim is an exceptionally fun time for children. How do we accentuate the excitement in our classrooms while not losing sight of some of Purim's important lessons?

## Purim – Four Mitzvot and Experiential Education

*February 2010*

> וַיִּכְתֹּב מָרְדֳּכַי אֶת-הַדְּבָרִים הָאֵלֶּה... לְקַיֵּם עֲלֵיהֶם לִהְיוֹת עֹשִׂים אֵת יוֹם
> אַרְבָּעָה עָשָׂר לְחֹדֶשׁ אֲדָר וְאֵת יוֹם-חֲמִשָּׁה עָשָׂר בּוֹ בְּכָל-שָׁנָה וְשָׁנָה :.....
> לַעֲשׂוֹת אוֹתָם יְמֵי מִשְׁתֶּה וְשִׂמְחָה וּמִשְׁלוֹחַ מָנוֹת אִישׁ לְרֵעֵהוּ וּמַתָּנוֹת
> לָאֶבְיֹנִים
>
> Mordecai charged the people to observe the fourteenth and fifteenth days of Adar every year....
> They were to observe them as days of feasting and merrymaking, and for the exchange of gifts
> of food and alms to the poor.
>
> **- The Book of Esther 9:20-22**

**Questions for Discussion:**

1. Jewish trivia quiz: what happens on the 14th day of the Hebrew month of Adar? So then what happens on the 15th? For bonus points, just what is Shushan Purim?

2. What is your favorite Purim tradition? If you have no favorite tradition, what are you most looking forward to learning about Purim?

3. Based on Mordecai's edict quoted above, we are commanded to do four mitzvot on Purim: 1. Tell the story, specifically by listening to the Book of Esther (*lishmoah megillah*) 2. Have a feast (*seudat mitzvah*) 3. Give gifts to friends and family (*mishloach manot*) 4. Give tzedakah and gifts to the poor. (*matanot laevyonim*). As a staff, discuss all four mitzvot so every person understands each one more than he or she did before. There is lots of information to be found in <u>Jewish Every Day</u> and all over the internet, including http://www.uscj.org/seabd/SynagogueResourceCtr/PURIM.pdf. Once everyone has a good understanding of each mitzvah, chose at least one to do together as a staff. Have a really joyful time celebrating a new mitzvah in a new way.

4. In his 2009 study, "Schools That Work," Jack Wertheimer found that "good schools create opportunities for students to engage in *experiential Jewish education*. By participating in actual prayer, ...engaging in activities to help the poor and needy, participating in programs celebrating Israel, students are exposed to Jewish experiences that they may long remember and may stimulate them to explore questions of personal meaning. This experiential component, in tandem with formal learning, is vital, as it provides students with the opportunity to live their Judaism and not only to learn about it." How will you create opportunities for your children and your families to authentically experience some or all of the mitzvot of Purim?

## Vashti and Esther

*March 2008*

> When Vashti is called to come to the king clad only in her crown (and, readers are to assume, nothing else), she refuses. The king is convinced by his advisors that all other women will learn to refuse their husbands as she did if he allows her to get away with it so he has her removed. Her time on stage is completed in less than a chapter.
>
> Since the 1970s, feminists have taken Vashti to heart as the first proto-feminist: She is the first woman in the Bible who refuses to be objectified as a sex object, instead naming such behavior as inappropriate.....
>
> What a contrast to Esther, who is quite meek in comparison. When brought to the palace, she passively goes along with whatever the head eunuch plans for her. When she finally approaches the king, she wines and dines him before beseeching him, using every traditional feminine wile in the book, and rather effectively at that.
>
> In many ways, Vashti is the paradigmatic woman who won't take any garbage from the men around her, even if it costs her, which it does. In comparison, I always thought of Esther as the ideal of the savvy female business exec who learns how to make it in the top tier of a man's world and bring her people along with her..... These have been the two models for how women have negotiated their lack of real power throughout history.
>
> **- Rabbi Susan Grossman, posting on** http://blog.beliefnet.com/virtualtalmud/2007/02/is-hillary-next-vashti.html

**Questions for Discussion:**

1. What do you know about Vashti and Esther from the Purim story? As a group, share what you all know to get a full picture. You can always check your facts in Megillat Esther (the Book of Esther).

2. Do you see yourself as more of a Vashti or more of an Esther? Why? Think about the children in your class. Which of them have the "take the bull by the horns" approach, and which use different resources and strategize?

3. Traditional commentators accused Vashti of not wanting to appear before the king because she had grown a tail or contracted leprosy. The rabbis of old were not big Vashti fans, to put it mildly. But in recent decades Vashti has been recast as a feminist, a strong woman with her head and her heart in the right place. Esther, on the other hand, works within the system, but also takes matters into her own hands when the going gets tough. How might you defend Vashti's actions, or not? Do you approve of Esther's tactics?

4. Do you include Vashti in your telling of the Purim story with your children? At what age do you believe it is appropriate to introduce children to Vashti? Remember, it is important never to teach children things they must unlearn later. This means you can edit the story but never change it. Make sure you have school-wide agreement about who is telling which version of the story. Both Vashti and Esther have valuable lessons for children – Vashti is an example of always standing up for what is right; Esther pays attention, she understands the people around her and she is wise, and brave, enough to use this understanding to shape events to her purposes. How can you give the children in your class lessons from both of Purim's heroines?

## Jews as Victims or Not

April 2006

---

"A short summary of every Jewish holiday: They tried to kill us. We won. Let's eat."

**- Comedian Alan King**

---

**Questions for Discussion:**

1. We've recently celebrated Hanukah and Purim and are now approaching Pesach, so the Alan King joke certainly strikes a chord. Refresh your memory – who is the "they" in each of these holidays? Who is the corresponding hero who saves us?

2. How does this "joke" make you feel? Do you agree with it? Do you disagree? What does this joke make you think about? What does it make you want to change in the world?

3. Consider the following snippets from the Pesach story:

   Then Pharaoh charged all his people, saying, *"Every boy that is born you shall throw into the Nile, but let every girl live"* (Exodus 1:22).

   *[And the Lord continued,] "Come, therefore, I will send you to Pharaoh, and you shall free My people, the Israelites, from Egypt." But Moses said to God, "Who am I that I should go to Pharaoh and free the Israelites from Egypt?"* (Exodus 3:10-11).

   *Then Miriam the prophetess, Aaron's sister, took a timbrel in her hand, and all the women went out after her in dance with timbrels.* (Exodus 15:20)

   What allows one person to victimize another? What gives someone the strength to overcome persecution? What do these verses tell you about Judaism and God? Who are some of the other Pesach heroes in Exodus chapters 1-15 (beyond Moses and Miriam)?

4. Many people struggle with this theme, with the Jewish people being seen as constantly having to fight for our survival and often being portrayed as victims. This can be especially true for people who work with young children. With this in mind, how can we still *truthfully* portray the story of Pesach (or any other similar holiday story) to our children, and still keep it within a positive light?

---

## Bedikat Chametz

*March 2007*

> "Any chametz or leaven that is in my possession which I have not seen, have not removed and do not know about, should be annulled and become ownerless, like the dust of the earth."
>
> **- From the declaration one says after the search for Chametz**

### Questions for Discussion:

1. Pesach is likely the most extensively prepared-for holiday on the Jewish calendar. After all the physical cleaning is done, we add a symbolic preparation too, with Bedikat Chametz, the search for chametz – leavened or not kosher-for-Pesach-food. Have you ever done Bedikat Chametz in your own home? Share stories of previous years' searches.

2. Pesach can be a time to rid not only our homes but also our souls of chametz. In CLAL's National Jewish Resource Center, there is a ceremony for Spring-Cleaning the Soul for Passover. We each harbor hidden sins, petty pride, and stubborn self-importance. When we look inside ourselves and take time to recognize and name the ways we oppress and have been oppressed, then we are able to take steps to rid ourselves of this "spiritual chametz" and move closer to our fullest freedom. Take a few moments for each person to write down some personal chametz. Share if you choose. Then crumple the paper up and toss it out. For the biggest effect, toss the notes into an empty coffee can and burn them. You can find the full ceremony at http://www.clal.org/rl42.html

3. The Torah requires that chametz not be eaten, or seen, nor even present in your house during Pesach (Exodus 13:3, 7, 15). All yeast-based baked goods must be removed from our premises (Exodus 12:15). The rabbis then detailed the process of removing the chametz. The declaration we make once we've found all the hidden chametz was written in Aramaic, the vernacular of the Jewish people at the time. Today we are told to be sure to make the declaration in a language we can understand. We essentially say, "We looked, we tried, but if we didn't find everything, we are not accountable." Why would the rabbis have created such a ceremony? What is the significance of being able to say to God "We did our best," and have that be absolutely good enough?

4. Young children love to play hide and go seek. Bedikat Chametz is hide and go seek in a Jewish context. How can we help children experience it as more than just a fun game of "search for the bread crumbs," and appreciate some of the deeper implications of Bedikat Chametz?

Slightly different versions of the entire bedikat chametz ritual can be found at:

- http://www.njop.org/html/Passoverwritings.html#BC

- http://www.milechai.com/text2/bedikat-chametz-kits.html

## Pesach

*March 2009*

---

*A midrash on the parting of the Sea of Reeds as the Jews fled from Egypt:* R. Judah said to R. Meir...One tribe said, "I will not be the first to go into the sea"; and another tribe also said, "I will not be the first to go into the sea." While they were standing there deliberating, Nachshon the son of Aminadab sprang forward and was the first to go down into the sea.

**- Babylonian Talmud,** *Sotah* **36b-37a**

---

*Recommended Prerequisite: To enhance this month's discussion, read Exodus 13:17-14:31, the story of the exodus from Egypt.*

**Questions for Discussion:**

1.  During the parting of the Red Sea we are introduced to Nachshon. In Exodus 14:16 we read, "And you raise your staff and stretch out your hand over the sea and split it, and the children of Israel shall come in the midst of the sea on dry land." The commentators questioned: How is it possible to be on dry ground and in the midst of the sea simultaneously? From this, some commentators gathered that the Israelites first had to enter the sea before the waters were able to split. (Student Rabbi Elana Sondel http://www.liberaljudaism.org/writtenword_thoughts_beshalach_ES.htm) How else might you interpret Exodus 14:16?

2.  Nachshon's actions were very brave. When have you (or someone you know) been brave, taking that first step when no one else dared?

3.  In the Talmud, the text above is Rabbi Judah's version of what happened. R. Judah offers his version in response to Rabbi Meir, who said that when the Jewish people got to the sea, each tribe wanted to be the first to go into the water. While they were arguing about who would be first, the tribe of Benjamin jumped forward and ran into the sea. The tribe of Judah was so mad, they started throwing stones at the tribe of Benjamin. This poses many questions. Which version is right? Why are there different versions? Other stories have different versions, too. Read *Joseph Had a Little Overcoat* by Simms Taback, *Bit by Bit* by Steve Sanfield and *Something From Nothing* by Phoebe Gilman. Same story, different versions. What can you and your children make of that?

4.  As you prepare for Passover, invite your children to ask questions about the things that don't make sense to them. Share the midrash of Nachshon as an answer to something the rabbis wondered about. Wonder with the children, "Do you think Nachshon was scared?" "What might have happened if Nachshon had not been so brave?"

5.  Rabbi Joe Black wrote a song about Nachshon ben Aminadav, called "Nachshon," on his album *Everyone's Got a Little Music.* This song is a modern midrash about Nachshon. Play this song for your children and talk about what they think happened there at the sea.

---

# Women of Pesach/Kos Miriam

*April 2008*

וַתָּשֶׂם בָּהּ אֶת-הַיֶּלֶד וַתָּשֶׂם בַּסּוּף עַל-שְׂפַת הַיְאֹר : וַתֵּתַצַּב
אֲחֹתוֹ מֵרָחֹק לְדֵעָה מַה-יֵּעָשֶׂה לוֹ

She put the child into it [the ark/basket] and placed it among the reeds by the bank of the Nile. And his sister [Miriam] stationed herself at a distance, to learn what would befall him.

**- Exodus 2:3-4**

וַתָּמָת שָׁם מִרְיָם וַתִּקָּבֵר שָׁם : וְלֹא-הָיָה מַיִם לָעֵדָה

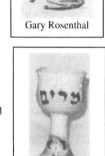

Gary Rosenthal

Miriam died there and was buried there, and the community was without water.

**- Numbers 20:1-2**

Rashi (11th Century, France) noticed the strange juxtaposition of Miriam's death and the shortage of water, and assumed that there must be a connection between the two. "From this we learn that all forty years, they had a well because of the merit of Miriam."

Irene Helitzer

**- Rabbi Bradley Shavit Artson, "Miriam--Water Under the Bridge?"**
http://www.myjewishlearning.org/texts/Weekly_Torah_Commentary/hukkat_artson5762.htm

## Questions for Discussion:

1. Miriam was the sister of Aaron and Moses, and she holds an important place in the Pesach story. Besides guarding her baby brother as he floats down the Nile and securing a job for her mother as the baby's nursemaid once the Pharaoh's daughter has found him, Miriam leads the women in dance and song once the Israelites have escaped Egypt and crossed the Sea of Reeds. What else do you know about Miriam?

2. Pictured above are two examples of a Kos Miriam (Miriam's Cup), which in recent years has gained popularity as another ritual for Pesach. The Kos Miriam is filled with water, as the Torah text and midrashim connect Miriam to water in many ways. Have you ever put or seen a Kos Miriam on a seder table? Share stories of the Kos Miriam and the rituals surrounding it. (If no one in your group has personal experience with a Kos Miriam, you can find lots of information at http://www.miriamscup.com).

3. The story of Passover would be impossible without the women. In addition to Miriam, Yocheved – Moses' mother, Shifra and Puah – the midwives who refused to kill the Israelite babies, Bat Paroh – Pharaoh's daughter, Tzipporah – Moses' wife, and the

Israelite women all contributed to our liberation from Egypt. Tell the stories of these women. If you're not sure of the details, check out Exodus chapters 1 and 2. There's also an article with lots of good details at http://www.morim.org/Contents.aspx?id=2059.

4. Why are Miriam and the other women important to young children? How will you insure that your children learn their stories, and not just Moses'? Miriam was a prophetess who danced; Shifra and Puah stood up for the right thing; Yocheved loved her child fiercely. How will you plan to incorporate these elements into your class's Passover preparations?

## Counting the Omer

*March 2010*

---

וּסְפַרְתֶּם לָכֶם מִמָּחֳרַת הַשַּׁבָּת מִיּוֹם הֲבִיאֲכֶם אֶת-**עֹמֶר** הַתְּנוּפָה שֶׁבַע שַׁבָּתוֹת תְּמִימֹת תִּהְיֶינָה: עַד מִמָּחֳרַת הַשַּׁבָּת הַשְּׁבִיעֹת תִּסְפְּרוּ חֲמִשִּׁים יוֹם

From the day after the sabbath [the first day of Pesach, not Shabbat], the day that you bring the sheaf of wave-offering [*omer*], you shall keep count until seven full weeks have elapsed: you shall count fifty days until the day after the seventh week.

**- Leviticus 23:15-16**

---

### Questions for Discussion:

1. As if Pesach wasn't a crazy enough time, we have to start counting the omer at the second seder. What is an omer? What happens on the fiftieth day? What's with all the counting, anyway? What other things do we count in Judaism? For answers to some of these questions, go to http://www.jewfaq.org/holidayb.htm. So you don't forget to count, go to http://www.uscj.org/images/OMER70.pdf for an omer calendar for 2010.

2. Have you ever remembered to count every day of the omer? If so, how did you do it? If not, why is it so hard to remember to do this mitzvah?

3. *Sifrat ha-omer*, or the period of counting the omer, is a time of preparation for receiving the Torah at Mount Sinai. United Synagogue suggests some questions to help us be more intentional about the counting. For example, "Long ago, Jews brought a certain measure of barley (an omer) to the Temple each day as an offering to God. What kind of offering might you make today?" (day 2) or "Think about the preparations that culminated in the celebration of Pesach this year. Do the rules, rituals, and restrictions associated with this holiday enhance your celebration? How?" (day 3) or "Shavuot celebrates the giving of the Torah on Mount Sinai. According to legend, this mountain was selected because of its small size and modesty. What can we learn from this?" (day 13) Choose one or two of these questions to discuss as a staff now, or choose a different question from the complete list at http://www.uscj.org/Counting_the_Omer_an6375.html.

4. What creative ways can you think of to count the omer with your children? How will it look different for two-year-olds than for four-year-olds? How can you prepare your children for counting the omer as you get ready for Pesach? What do you want your children to learn from counting the omer? (Go beyond math skills.)

---

## Birkat Hachama

*April 2009*

While most staff meeting shiurim are designed to be used at any time during the month, this month's shiur focuses on an event we have the opportunity to participate in on April 8, 2009.

> יד וַיֹּאמֶר אֱ-לֹהִים יְהִי מְאֹרֹת בִּרְקִיעַ הַשָּׁמַיִם לְהַבְדִּיל בֵּין הַיּוֹם וּבֵין הַלָּיְלָה... : טו וְהָיוּ לִמְאוֹרֹת בִּרְקִיעַ הַשָּׁמַיִם לְהָאִיר עַל-הָאָרֶץ וַיְהִי-כֵן : טז וַיַּעַשׂ אֱ-לֹהִים אֶת-שְׁנֵי הַמְּאֹרֹת הַגְּדֹלִים .... : יז וַיִּתֵּן אֹתָם אֱ-לֹהִים בִּרְקִיעַ הַשָּׁמָיִם לְהָאִיר עַל-הָאָרֶץ : יח וְלִמְשֹׁל בַּיּוֹם וּבַלַּיְלָה וּלְהַבְדִּיל בֵּין הָאוֹר וּבֵין הַחֹשֶׁךְ
>
> On the fourth day of creation: God said, "Let there be lights in the expanse of the sky to separate day from night....and they shall serve as lights in the expanse of the sky to shine upon the earth." And it was so. God made the two great lights...and God set them in the expanse of the sky to shine upon the earth, to dominate the day and the night, and to separate light from darkness. - **Genesis 1:14-18**

**Questions for Discussion:**

1. What does the sun mean to you? How does the sun affect your daily life?

2. Birkat HaChamah, the blessing for the sun, is only recited once every 28 years, at the very beginning of the full solar cycle. This moment will happen on April 8, 2009. This opportunity to bless the sun marks the time when the sun returns to the exact place in the sky where it was when it was formed, at the first hour of the night before the fourth day. The ritual can take place outside, early in the morning, just as the sun rises, just as we see the first glint of gold on the horizon, or it could also be later in the morning as you greet your children at school. The ceremony could be a scholarly experience with readings from psalms and the Talmud, or it could include drums, a little yoga, and the singing of "Here Comes the Sun" by the Beatles. Either way, the official blessing we say over the sun's return to its birthplace is the same blessing we say over other awe-filled moments, such as seeing lightening or shooting stars or experiencing an earthquake:

   *Baruch Atah Adonai, Eloheinu Melech HaOlam, Oseh Ma-aseh Bereishit.*

   If it were up to you to bless the sun, how would you do it? What would you include?

3. Even with all the preparations for Passover going on (Birkat HaChamah happens the morning of the first seder), how might you take this opportunity to create a special moment of connection for your children and families? After all, they won't get another chance to greet the sun in its original position for another 28 years.

For more information, see http://www.blessthesun.org/tiki-index.php.

## Israel/Yom Ha'atzmaut

*April 2007*

---

Accordingly we, members of the People's Council, representatives of the Jewish community of Eretz-Israel and of the Zionist movement, are here assembled on the day of the termination of the British mandate over Eretz-Israel and, by virtue of our natural and historic right and on the strength of the resolution of the United Nations General Assembly, hereby declare the establishment of a Jewish state in Eretz-Israel, to be known as the State of Israel.

**- From the Declaration of The Establishment of The State Of Israel, 5th day of Iyar, 5708 (14th May, 1948)**

---

**Questions for Discussion:**

1. The creation of the State of Israel is grounded in history and memory, so much so that Yom Ha'Atzmaut (Israeli Independence Day) is immediately preceded on the calendar by Yom Ha'Zikaron (Memorial Day). Unlike their American counterparts, almost every Israeli family has lost someone in a battle for the existence of Israel; keeping that in mind, discuss the reasons for the juxtaposition of these two days on the calendar and what the resulting affect (not a typo, but the emotional outcome) is on the Israeli and Jewish people.

2. If you have been to Israel, describe the most enduring moments you experienced there. If you have not been to Israel, describe the thing about it that sounds most enticing to you.

3. Here are the words to Israel's national anthem, Hatikvah (The Hope):

| | | |
|---|---|---|
| *As long as the Jewish spirit is yearning deep in the heart With eyes turned toward the East, looking toward Zion,* | *Kol ode balevav P'nimah – Nefesh Yehudi homiyah Ulfa'atey mizrach kadimah Ayin l'tzion tzofiyah.* | כָּל עוֹד בַּלֵּבָב פְּנִימָה, נֶפֶשׁ יְהוּדִי הוֹמִיָּה. וּלְפַאֲתֵי מִזְרָח קָדִימָה עַיִן לְצִיּוֹן צוֹפִיָּה. |
| *Then our hope - the two-thousand-year-old hope -* | *Ode lo avdah tikvatenu Hatikvah bat shnot alpayim: L'hiyot am chofshi b'artzenu* | עוֹד לֹא אָבְדָה תִּקְוָתֵנוּ, הַתִּקְוָה בַּת שְׁנוֹת אַלְפַּיִם, |
| *will not be lost: To be a free people in our land, The land of Zion and Jerusalem.* | *Eretz Tzion v'Yerushalayim.* | לִהְיוֹת עַם חָפְשִׁי בְּאַרְצֵנוּ, אֶרֶץ צִיּוֹן וִירוּשָׁלָיִם. |

What dreams and goals are expressed in this song? What does Hatikvah tell you about the Jewish people and our relationship to the land of Israel?

---

4. We recognize that the concept of "country" is impossible for very young children to understand. So when we teach about Israel, we must remember that we are striving to create a love for Israel that will become part of the foundation of each child's Jewish identity. As they grow, they will "own" Israel as someplace precious to them, a familiar place they seek to visit and always to support. How can you create experiences for children that truly connect them to Israel at the foundational level, both in celebration of Yom Ha'Atzmaut and through the year?

## Other Information:

- The entire text of the Declaration of the State of Israel can be found at http://www.mfa.gov.il/MFA/

- To listen to Hatikvah, go to http://www.stateofisrael.com/anthem/

## Lag B'Omer/Study of Torah

*May 2006*

---

**A story from the Talmud for Lag B'Omer (Berachot 61b):**

Rabbi Akiva lived during the time after Judea had been conquered by the Romans. Even though the Roman rulers had made it illegal to study Torah, Rabbi Akiba kept his school open and continued to teach his students.

One day someone said to him "Akiva, why do you break the Roman law by teaching Torah? Do you wish to be imprisoned – or worse?"

Akiva answered him with this story: , Once as a fox was walking alongside a river, he saw fish going in swarms from one place to another. He said to them, "What are you fleeing from?" They replied, "From the nets cast for us by human beings." The hungry fox said to them, "Would you like to come up on the dry land so that you and I can live together in the way that my ancestors lived with your ancestors?" They replied, "Are you the one that they call the cleverest of animals? Rather than being clever, you are foolish. If we are afraid in the element in which we live, how much more in the element where we would die!"

Rabbi Akiva then explained: "So it is with us. As fish surely will die without water, so the Jewish people surely will die without the Torah." As water is home to the fish, Torah is home to us.

---

**Questions for Discussion:**

1. Why is the Torah important to the Jewish people?

2. What are some of the things in your life that you need in order to survive (or to continue to be you)?

3. We tell this story on Lag B'Omer (the 33rd day of the Omer, the seven weeks between Pesach and Shavuot) because one of the things Lag B'Omer commemorates is the day a plague, or perhaps the siege of the Romans, was lifted against Rabbi Akiva's students. What Jewish values can we take from this story?

4. The story certainly teaches us about the importance of Talmud Torah, the study of Torah, to the Jewish people. How can you weave this value into your classroom throughout the year, and especially on Lag B'Omer and as your children leave your school for the summer?

---

## Standing at Sinai/Connection to Torah

*May 2007*

My brother and I were at Sinai
He kept a journal
of what he saw
of what he heard
of what it all meant to him

I wish I had such a record
of what happened to me there

It seems like every time I want to write
I can't
I'm always holding a baby
one of my own
or one for a friend
always holding a baby
so my hands are never free
to write things down

And then
As time passes
The particulars
The hard data
The who what when where why
Slip away from me
And all I'm left with is
The feeling

But feelings are just sounds
The vowel barking of a mute

My brother is so sure of what he heard
After all he's got a record of it
Consonant after consonant after consonant

If we remembered it together
We could recreate holy time
Sparks flying

**- Merle Feld, "We All Stood Together,"**
***A Spiritual Life: A Jewish Feminist Journey***
**[Albany: SUNY Press, 2007], p. 245**

### Questions for Discussion:

1.  In recounting when we stood together at Sinai, receiving the Torah, we are told, "But take utmost care and watch yourselves scrupulously, so that you do not forget the things that you saw with your own eyes and so that they do not fade from your mind as long as you live. Make them known to your children and to your children's children" (Deuteronomy 4:9). Merle Feld's poem points out that this attention, this memory, is not always possible. How do we reconcile the disparity between our desire to preserve and document a moment and the reality of fleeting moments and demanding priorities?

2.  The Torah tells us, "I make this covenant…not with you alone, but both with those who are standing here with us this day… and with those who are not with us here this day." (Deuteronomy 29:13) We all stood at Sinai. The giving of the Torah was intended for each of our ears. Picture yourself standing at Sinai. Are you young, struggling with a baby on your hip, or are you an old woman at the end of her days? Did you come straight from work with paint shmeared on your pants?

3.  When we each envision ourselves standing at Sinai, we can each embark on our own connection to the Torah. We want children to have a sense that they, too, stood at Sinai, so that they can take ownership of the Torah, all the stories and the laws. Still, very young children are very literal. How can you enable children to experience standing at Sinai, while at the same time actually use the experience to give children a connection to Torah?

## Ruth/Shavuot

*May 2008*

> וַתֹּאמֶר רוּת אַל-תִּפְגְּעִי-בִי לְעָזְבֵךְ לָשׁוּב מֵאַחֲרָיִךְ כִּי אֶל-אֲשֶׁר תֵּלְכִי אֵלֵךְ
> וּבַאֲשֶׁר תָּלִינִי אָלִין עַמֵּךְ עַמִּי וֵא-לֹהַיִךְ אֱ-לֹהָי
>
> But Ruth replied, "Do not urge me to leave you, to turn back and not follow you. For wherever you go, I will go; wherever you lodge, I will lodge; your people will be my people, and your God my God."
>
> **- Ruth 1:16**

### Questions for Discussion:

1. We read the story of Ruth on Shavuot*. While many schools will have wrapped up the school year before then this year, there are important lessons to take from Ruth as we send our families off, or switch gears, over the summer. Make sure the entire staff knows the story of Ruth – tell the story together, or read it from the Tanach (in the Ketuvim/Writings section) or from a child's version such as *The Story of Ruth* by Maxine Rose Schur (Kar Ben).

2. Ruth chooses to throw her lot in with the Jewish people. It is our goal that, at least in part due to the wonderful experience they have in our school, our children and families will choose to do the same. Discuss some experiences your children and families have had over the year that have connected them to the Jewish community and to Jewish life. What are some ways your school can continue to connect your families to Jewish life as they leave your program, either for the summer or for good?

3. At the end of the book of Ruth, Ruth gives birth to a son, but her mother-in-law, "Naomi, took the child and held it to her bosom. She became its nurse, and the women neighbors gave him a name, saying, 'A son is born to Naomi!'" (Ruth 4:16-17). This serves to remind us that not just the child but the parents and even the grandparents are integral participants in the educational experiences that happen in our school. How have you met parents' adult learning needs this year? How can your school, perhaps in conjunction with the synagogue or other community institutions, come to be known as a place where everyone, not just young children, can come to learn?

4. What are some Jewish things to do around town this summer? (Even a picnic in the park is a Jewish thing to do if you say a blessing before starting to eat!) Let your families know some things they can do, and have fun!

## Continuing Jewish Learning/Shavuot

*May 2010*

---

"The Torah is sweet, the blintzes are sweet," Sarah sang that afternoon as she washed Mrs. Grossinger's sheets. She winked at Natie. "We have some blintzes to make – and soon."

"Blitzes, blintzes, a mountain of blintzes!" Natie chanted.

"Ach! What a boy! You remembered. A mountain of blintzes to make us think of the mountain Moses climbed. Up and down he went, to bring us the Torah, the Laws."

**- From *A Mountain of Blintzes* by Barbara Diamond Goldin, Marshall Cavendish, 2010**

---

**Questions for Discussion:**

1. Shavuot is a culmination of many things -- of counting the omer, of the grain harvest, of waiting at Sinai for Moses to come down, of the yearly cycle of holidays. Shavuot also marks beginnings -- of our life as the Jewish people, of a life with Torah. How is the school year culminating right now? At the same time, what potential beginnings are also in the air?

2. A blintz is a crepe-like pancake that is folded around a filling, most often cheese-based, but sometimes fruit such as blueberry or apple. What are your favorite kinds of blintzes? Your choice for toppings? Have a great recipe for blintzes? If you've never tasted a blintz, be sure to "acquire a friend and a teacher" and secure yourself an invitation to someone's home or classroom to eat some.

3. According to a study done in 2002, "nearly 70 percent of the interviewed families were 'doing something different' as a result of their child's Jewish preschool experience. Jewish ritual and lifestyle changes included lighting Shabbat candles, joining a synagogue and deciding to send a child to a Jewish day school." (Pearl Beck, "Jewish Preschools as Gateways to Jewish Life," *Contact Magazine*, Autumn 2002.) As you celebrate Shavuot and the high point of connection to Torah with your children, focus also on the connection to Torah and Jewish learning for the entire family. If you need ideas, check out the Family Education and Learning section in the Vision for Conservative Early Childhood Programs, http://uscj.org/images/ECE_vision.pdf.

4. One reason for eating blintzes (and other dairy foods) on Shavuot is because the Torah is likened to milk and honey. "Honey and milk are under your tongue" (Song of Songs 4:11). How can you bring the blintzes, and the sweetness of the Torah, both literally and figuratively, to the children in your classroom?

---

# More Holidays

## Shabbat/Bereshit

*October 2006*

> וַיְכַל אֱ-לֹהִים בַּיּוֹם הַשְּׁבִיעִי מְלַאכְתּוֹ אֲשֶׁר עָשָׂה וַיִּשְׁבֹּת בַּיּוֹם הַשְּׁבִיעִי
> מִכָּל-מְלַאכְתּוֹ אֲשֶׁר עָשָׂה : וַיְבָרֶךְ אֱ-לֹהִים אֶת-יוֹם הַשְּׁבִיעִי וַיְקַדֵּשׁ אֹתוֹ כִּי
> בוֹ שָׁבַת מִכָּל-מְלַאכְתּוֹ אֲשֶׁר-בָּרָא אֱ-לֹהִים לַעֲשׂוֹת
>
> On the seventh day God finished the work that He had been doing, and He rested on the
> seventh day from all the work that He had done. And God blessed the seventh day and
> declared it holy, because on it God rested from all the work of creation that He had done.
>
> **- Genesis 2:2-3**

**Questions for Discussion:**

1. The Hebrew name used by Jews for the seventh day is Shabbat from the verb *lish-bote*,
   to rest), which appears twice in the passage above (enlarged in different conjugations).
   What does this tell us about what's important about the seventh day for Jews?

2. The Ten Commandments appear twice in the Torah, in Exodus 20:2-14 and in
   Deuteronomy 5:6-18. The fourth commandment begins: *"Remember the day of Shabbat
   and keep it holy."* (In Deuteronomy it says "Observe the day of Shabbat and keep it
   holy.") In Exodus 31:17 we are told *"on the seventh day God ceased/rested from work
   and was refreshed."* Why is Shabbat so important that observing it is one of the Ten
   Commandments? What are some ways we might be refreshed by Shabbat? What are
   some things you know of that people are supposed to do or not do on Shabbat? How do
   those things meet the Shabbat values of resting or being refreshed?

   How do you remember or observe Shabbat? (Please remember that Shabbat
   observance, like most of Jewish life, is not an all-or-nothing proposition. Every Jew
   celebrates or remembers Shabbat differently. There is no right or wrong if a person is
   actively making choices about how to observe Shabbat.) If you observe a Sabbath that
   is not the day of Shabbat, what does your observance of the "day of rest" consist of? We
   all know that we are too busy. How does your Shabbat or Sabbath help you become
   refreshed? If it doesn't, what changes might you make in your life to incorporate a holy
   rest into your routine? (Think small changes to start with!)

3. We celebrate Shabbat because God rested on the seventh day of creation. That rest
   was holy (and needed) because of all the creating that God did on the preceding six
   days. It is impossible to understand the holiness of Shabbat rest without first exploring
   the phenomenon of creation (found in the first chapter of Genesis). How can you help
   your children to better understand creation so as to enhance their understanding and
   love of Shabbat? How will that look different for two-year-olds than it does for four-year-
   olds?

# Thanksgiving

*November 2006*

---

"So here we are now, safe in America. God first brought the Pilgrims and then He brought us, the Jews. The Pilgrims were the first to give thanks to Him, but I believe we also owe Him a Thanksgiving. As much as anybody, we owe Him thanks."

One of the Rabbis leaned forward and asked, "In what manner is this thanks given?"

"From what my teacher told me, it sounds something like a seder, Rabbi. Family and friends sit down together, offer a prayer of thanks, and then they eat together."

Two weeks later, Rivka served the food for the first Thanksgiving on Hester Street.

**- From *Rivka's First Thanksgiving* by Elsa Okon Rael, McElderry Books, 2001**

---

**Questions for Discussion:**

1. Is Thanksgiving a Jewish holiday? Is Thanksgiving an ok holiday for Jews?

2. What are your favorite memories of Thanksgiving celebrations or traditions? Who do you celebrate Thanksgiving with?

3. Some historians suggest that the first Thanksgiving feast was based on the holiday of Sukkot. This makes sense, given what we know of the Pilgrims as a deeply religious people who may very well have looked to the Bible (Leviticus 23:33). "They knew that Sukkot was an autumn harvest festival, and there is evidence that they fashioned the first Thanksgiving after the Jewish custom of celebrating the success of the year's crops." says Gloria Kaufer Greene, author of the *New Jewish Holiday Cookbook* (Times Books). In what other ways are Sukkot and Thanksgiving similar?

4. How might you weave the connection to Sukkot into the celebration of Thanksgiving in your classroom? When teaching Thanksgiving, consider the "big ideas" or "enduring understandings" – what really is the most important thing you want your children to remember about Thanksgiving? Is it about Pilgrims and Indians? Is it what turkeys say? Or it is something deeper, more central to their lives as members of a community and as Jews?

**Have a happy Thanksgiving, full of blessings!**

---

## Rosh Chodesh

*January 2010*

---

וּבְרָאשֵׁי חָדְשֵׁכֶם וּתְקַעְתֶּם בַּחֲצֹצְרֹת עַל עֹלֹתֵיכֶם.....

....And in the beginnings of your new months you shall blow with the trumpets over your burnt offerings.....

- **Numbers 10:10**

---

**Questions for Discussion:**

1.  What do you on a monthly basis that feeds your soul, or rejuvenates you, or connects you to others, or to yourself, in a positive way?

2.  Traditionally, Rosh Chodesh, literally "head of the month," the marking of the new Jewish month with the sighting of the first sliver of the new moon, has been a women's holiday, observed in ancient times by women refraining from work, and in recent decades by women's groups gathering with song, prayer, and storytelling. The assignment of Rosh Chodesh as a women's holiday is attributed to a midrash. When Moses brought the Israelite people to Mount Sinai, he left them waiting at the bottom of the mountain while he went up to the top to speak with God and receive the Torah. While Moses was away, the people panicked, fearing that he would never return and that they would be left, deserted in the wilderness to die (Exodus 32). They demanded that Aaron, Moses' brother and right-hand man, build a golden calf to worship for them. According to the midrash, the women did not contribute to this panic, and indeed refused to give up their jewelry to the building of an idol. As a reward for those women's faith, God granted all women the holiday of Rosh Chodesh, so that like the moon women would be rejuvenated each month.

    Are you familiar with the holiday of Rosh Chodesh? Do you know of any women's Rosh Chodesh groups? What do they do to celebrate Rosh Chodesh?

3.  As we well know, young children do not yet grasp time concepts as broad as "week," "month," or "year." Do you have a calendar in your classroom that you fill in with the children as the month progresses? What are your learning goals for your children with regard to the calendar? Is "doing calendar" the most developmentally appropriate way to achieve these goals? How else could you meet them?

4.  Celebrating Rosh Chodesh with children each month connects them to the cyclical nature of Judaism (the same way celebrating Shabbat each week does, but in a slightly longer cycle). Children come to see the moon as a Jewish timekeeper: new moon at Rosh Hashanah, full moon at Tu B'Shevat and the beginning of Pesach. For these reasons, Rosh Chodesh is a relevant and important holiday to celebrate with young children. How might you celebrate Rosh Chodesh in your class?*

---

# Jewish Values/Stories in the
# Torah and Beyond

## Teaching Noah in Early Childhood

*October 2009*

---

נֹחַ אִישׁ צַדִּיק תָּמִים הָיָה בְּדֹרֹתָיו אֶת-הָאֱ-לֹהִים הִתְהַלֶּךְ-נֹחַ

Noah was a righteous man; he was blameless in his age; Noah walked with God.

**- Genesis 6:9 JPS TANAKH 1999**

This is the story of Noah, a righteous man.

**-** *First Steps in Learning Torah with Young Children*, **narrative, Rivka Behar, et. al., BJE of Greater New York. 1993**

Noah was simple. Noah was good. Noah walked the way God wants people to walk.

**-** *A Child's Garden of Torah*, **Joel Lurie Grishaver, Torah Aura Productions, 1996**

---

**Please Note:** *This month's shiur requires some prep work. Gather all of the picture-book versions of the story of Noah that you can find. Look at early childhood Torah curriculum guides as well. A suggested bibliography can be found on the following page of this collection.*

**Questions for Discussion:**

1. As a staff, retell the story of Noah. Refer to Genesis, chapter 6:5-9:28, for the original text. Spend a little time talking through the challenging or unfamiliar parts.

2. What are the most important things for young children to learn from, and about, the story of Noah? What are the big ideas that are relevant to two-year-olds? Threes? Fours?

3. Look through the books you collected. Pay attention to what the illustrations say, how true the story is to the original text, what the big ideas are in the books, and for what ages they are appropriate. As evidenced by the samples in the text box above, every translation is an interpretation. How does each book interpret the story?

4. Make a plan. How will the story of Noah be approached for each age group in a way that will appropriately expand children's understanding each year?

---

## Noah Resources for Early Childhood

### Torah curriculum resources

- Arcus, Lorraine, *Torah Alive*, New York: URJ Press, 2004. Also available – *Torah Alive! Parent Connection.* http://www.urjpress.com

- Behar, Rivka, Floreva Cohen and Ruth Musnikow, *First Steps in Learning Torah With Young Jewish Children, Vols. 1 and II (Bereshit and Sh'mot)*, New York: Board of Jewish Education of Greater New York, 1993. http://www.bjeny.org

- Chubara, Yona, Miriam Feinberg, and Rena Rotenberg. *Torah Talk,* Denver, CO: A.R.E. Publishing, 1989. http://www.behrmanhouse.com

- Greenberg, Tobey, and Nechama Retting. *Morah Morah Teach Me Torah*, Los Angeles, Torah Aura Productions, 2009. http://www.torahaura.com

### Jewish Children's Bibles

- Frankel, Ellen, *JPS Illustrated Children's Bible*, Jewish Publication Society, 2009.

- Grishaver, Joel Lurie, *A Child's Garden of Torah*, Torah Aura Productions, 1996.

- Prenzlau, Sheryl, *The Jewish Children's Bible* (five volumes), Pitspopany Press, 1999.

### Noah Picture books

- Brett, Jan, *On Noah's Ark*, G.P. Putnam's Sons, 2003.

- Bruna, Dick, *Caleb's Ride on Noah's Ark*, Big Tent Entertainment, 2004.

- Coplestone, Lis, and Jim Coplestone, *Noah's Bed*, Frances Lincoln, 2004.

- Cousins, Lucy, *Noah's Ark*, Thomas Nelson, 1999.

- Figley, Marty Rhodes, *Noah's Wife*, Ferdmans, 1998.

- Gerstein, Mordicai, *Noah and the Great Flood*, Simon and Schuster, 1999.

- Greene, Rhonda Gowler, *Noah & the Mighty Ark*, Zonderkidz, 2007.

- Greengard, Alison, *Noah's Ark*, EKS, 2004.

- Jules, Jacqueline, *Noah and the Ziz*, Kar-Ben, 2005.

- Kuskin, Karla, *The Animals and the Ark*, Simon and Schuster, 2002.

- Lenski, Lois, *Mr. and Mrs. Noah*, Random House, 2002.

- Lepon, Shoshana, *Noah & the Rainbow*, Judaica Press, 1993.

- Le Tord, Bijou, *Noah's Trees,* Harper-Collins, 1999

- Ludwig, Warren, *Old Noah's Elephants*, G.P. Putnam's Sons, 1991.

- Paley, Joan, *One More River: A Noah's Ark Counting Song*, Little Brown, 2002.

- Pigni, Guido, *The Story of the Giraffe*, Front Street, 2007.

- Pinnington, Andrea, *Sparkle and Shine Noah's Ark*, DK Publishing, 2008.

- Reid, Barbara*, Two By Two*, Scholastic, 1996.

- Reid, Barbara, *Fox Walked Alone*, Albert Whitman & Company, 2009.

- Reinhart, Matthew, *The Ark*, Simon and Schuster, 2005.

- Rouss, Sylvia, *The Littlest Pair*, Pitspopany, 2001.

- Sasso, Sandy Eisenberg, *Naamah, Noah's Wife*, Jewish Lights, 2002.

- Singer, Isaac Bashevis, *Why Noah Chose the Dove*, Farrar, Straus and Giroux, 1973.

- Spier, Peter, *Noah's Ark*, Doubleday/Random House, 1977.

- Wilson, Anne, *Noah's Ark*, Chronicle Books, 2002.

The Noah picture books listed here are largely suggested on the AJL Jewish Values Finder, http://www.ajljewishvalues.org/index.htm Some of these titles are out of print, but all are available used from amazon.com and other on-line vendors.

Some other Noah titles are listed in the ForWordsBooks catalog at http://forwordsbooks.com/.

Even more suggestions can be found in *Jewish Every Day* by Maxine Segal Handelman, page 87.

And of course, there are hundreds of suggestions at www.amazon.com. Many Noah books are published by Christian publishers. It is worthwhile to check books for their religious slant before introducing them to children.

## Blessings /Lech Lecha

*October 2007*

| | |
|---|---|
| [Lech-lecha] The Lord spoke to Abram: "Go forth from your native land and from your father's house to the land that I will show you. I will make of you a great nation, And I will bless you; I will make your name great, And you shall be a blessing." — **Genesis 12:1-2** | ‏[פרשת לך לך] וַיֹּאמֶר ה' אֶל-אַבְרָם לֶךְ-לְךָ מֵאַרְצְךָ וּמִמּוֹלַדְתְּךָ וּמִבֵּית אָבִיךָ אֶל-הָאָרֶץ אֲשֶׁר אַרְאֶךָּ וְאֶעֶשְׂךָ לְגוֹי גָּדוֹל וַאֲבָרֶכְךָ וַאֲגַדְּלָה שְׁמֶךָ וֶהְיֵה בְּרָכָה |

### Questions for Discussion:

1.  Parashat Lech-lecha (the Torah portion Lech-lecha, Genesis 12:1-17:27) is full of blessings. God blesses Abram several times, even blessing him with a new name: Abraham (and his wife, Sarai, with a new name: Sarah)! King Melchizedek of Salem blesses Abram and his God, God blesses Hagar, foretelling the birth of Ishmael, and God blesses Ishmael, as well as foretells the birth of Isaac, promising that a covenant will be maintained with him. What does it mean to be blessed?

2.  What are some blessings in your life? In the passage above, God tells Abram that he will be a blessing. How are you a blessing?

3.  Most blessings start with the Hebrew phrase *Ba-ruch A-tah Adonai* -Blessed are You Lord." The word Ba-ruch/Bless has the same root as the Hebrew word Be-rech, which means "knee." Sometimes when we say a blessing, we actually bend our knees when we say "Ba-ruch," involving our entire body in the blessing. But even when we don't bend our knees, how does this bless-knee connection change the meaning of the blessings we say?

4.  The rabbis tell us we should say 100 blessings a day. Indeed, there are many standard times during the day for saying blessings, such as eating and during tefilla (prayer), as well as special times, such as during a thunder storm or upon seeing a flowering tree. When we engage in "God-talk," referring to God ("Look at the beautiful flower God created") or saying a blessing, we make a safe environment for young children to ask about God, thus creating their own relationships with God. What can we do if we happen upon a "blessable" moment but don't know the traditional blessing to say?

## Bikur Cholim/Abraham at the Tent

*November 2007*

---

בְּעֶצֶם הַיּוֹם הַזֶּה נִמּוֹל אַבְרָהָם וְיִשְׁמָעֵאל בְּנוֹ : וְכָל-אַנְשֵׁי בֵיתוֹ יְלִיד בָּיִת
וּמִקְנַת-כֶּסֶף מֵאֵת בֶּן-נֵכָר נִמֹּלוּ אִתּוֹ : וַיֵּרָא אֵלָיו יְהֹוָה בְּאֵלֹנֵי מַמְרֵא וְהוּא
יֹשֵׁב פֶּתַח-הָאֹהֶל כְּחֹם הַיּוֹם.

Thus Abraham and his son Ishmael were circumcised on that very day, and all his household;
his homeborn slaves and those that had been bought from outsiders, were circumcised with
him. The Lord appeared to him by the terebinths [small Mediterranean trees] of Mamre; he
[Abraham] was sitting at the entrance of the tent as the day grew hot.

**- Genesis 17:26-18:1**

---

**Questions for Discussion:**

1. It is said that the third day after circumcision is the most painful. The rabbis say that God
   visited Abraham on this day, and that God is establishing the model for *bikur cholim*
   (bee-kore ho-leem), the mitzvah of visiting the sick (*Sotah* 14a). What might you imagine
   God said or did with Abraham on this visit? With cold and flu season upon us, what are
   some things you can imagine saying or doing when you visit someone who is sick?

2. Have you ever been sick or injured, and had people visit, call or email you? Have people
   sent cards? How did it feel to receive these visits and messages? What does it feel like
   when you are the healthy person making the visit?

3. In the Talmud, we learn, "One who visits removes one sixtieth of the patient's illness."
   (*Nedarim* 39b) This attributes great power to the mitzvah of bikur cholim. How could this
   be true? Do you believe that receiving a visit actually can make someone who is sick or
   injured better?

4. Young children are very capable of doing the mitzvah of bikur cholim. The Talmud is
   clear on this point: "Bikur cholim has no boundaries or limits, i.e., youth may visit the
   elderly and the elderly may visit the youth" (*Nedarim* 39a). There are many ways to
   involve children. The class can call an absent child on the phone, or make and send
   cards in the mail. If the class has jobs, one job can be *Bikur Cholim* Helper. This child is
   responsible for noticing if all the children are present, and to point out if someone is
   missing. If a child is missing because s/he is sick, the *Bikur Cholim* Helper can call the
   child on the phone. How will bikur cholim become a regular practice in your classroom?

More information and resources about bikur cholim can be found at
http://www.bikurcholimcc.com/.

---

## Hachnasat Orchim/Abraham at the Tent

*November 2005*

וַיֵּרָא אֵלָיו ה' בְּאֵלֹנֵי מַמְרֵא וְהוּא יֹשֵׁב פֶּתַח-הָאֹהֶל כְּחֹם הַיּוֹם : וַיִּשָּׂא עֵינָיו
וַיַּרְא וְהִנֵּה שְׁלֹשָׁה אֲנָשִׁים נִצָּבִים עָלָיו וַיַּרְא וַיָּרָץ לִקְרָאתָם מִפֶּתַח הָאֹהֶל
וַיִּשְׁתַּחוּ אָרְצָה : וַיֹּאמַר אֲדֹנָי אִם-נָא מָצָאתִי חֵן בְּעֵינֶיךָ אַל-נָא תַעֲבֹר מֵעַל
עַבְדֶּךָ : יֻקַּח-נָא מְעַט-מַיִם וְרַחֲצוּ רַגְלֵיכֶם וְהִשָּׁעֲנוּ תַּחַת הָעֵץ : וְאֶקְחָה פַת-
לֶחֶם וְסַעֲדוּ לִבְּכֶם אַחַר תַּעֲבֹרוּ כִּי-עַל-כֵּן עֲבַרְתֶּם עַל-עַבְדְּכֶם וַיֹּאמְרוּ כֵּן תַּעֲשֶׂה
כַּאֲשֶׁר דִּבַּרְתָּ : וַיְמַהֵר אַבְרָהָם הָאֹהֱלָה אֶל-שָׂרָה וַיֹּאמֶר מַהֲרִי שְׁלֹשׁ סְאִים
קֶמַח סֹלֶת לוּשִׁי וַעֲשִׂי עֻגוֹת : וְאֶל-הַבָּקָר רָץ אַבְרָהָם וַיִּקַּח בֶּן-בָּקָר רַךְ וָטוֹב
וַיִּתֵּן אֶל-הַנַּעַר וַיְמַהֵר לַעֲשׂוֹת אֹתוֹ : וַיִּקַּח חֶמְאָה וְחָלָב וּבֶן-הַבָּקָר אֲשֶׁר עָשָׂה
וַיִּתֵּן לִפְנֵיהֶם וְהוּא עֹמֵד עֲלֵיהֶם תַּחַת הָעֵץ וַיֹּאכֵלוּ

"God appeared to him [Abraham] in the Plains of Mamre while he was sitting at the entrance of the tent in the heat of the day. [Abraham] lifted his eyes and saw: Behold! Three men were standing over him. He perceived, so he ran toward them from the entrance of his tent, and bowed toward the ground. And he said, 'My lord, if I find favor in your eyes, please do not go past your servant. Let some water be brought, and wash your feet, and recline beneath the tree. I will fetch a morsel of bread that you may sustain yourselves, then go on- inasmuch as you have passed your servant's way.' They said, 'Do so, just as you have said.'

"Abraham rushed to the tent to Sarah and said, 'Hurry! Three se'ahs [measures] of the finest flour! Knead and make cakes.' Then Abraham ran to the cattle, took a calf, tender and good, and gave it to the youth, who hurried to prepare it. He took curds and milk, and the calf that he prepared, and he placed these before them [his guests]. He stood over them beneath the tree and they ate."

**- Genesis 18:1-8**

### Questions for Discussion:

1. What actions did Abraham take?

2. What was his level of energy or enthusiasm? How do we know?

3. From this passage in Bereshit (Genesis) we get the Jewish value of hachnasat orchim (hospitality). What does this text teach us about how we should extend hospitality?

4. How is hachnasat orchim a part of your life?

5. How do we teach this value to young children, and make hachnasat orchim a living, vital part of our children's experience in our classrooms, and in our families' experience in our school?

# Hesed

*November 2008*

טו וַיְהִי-הוּא טֶרֶם כִּלָּה לְדַבֵּר וְהִנֵּה רִבְקָה יֹצֵאת אֲשֶׁר יֻלְּדָה לִבְתוּאֵל בֶּן-מִלְכָּה אֵשֶׁת נָחוֹר אֲחִי
אַבְרָהָם וְכַדָּהּ עַל-שִׁכְמָהּ: טז וְהַנַּעֲרָ טֹבַת מַרְאֶה מְאֹד בְּתוּלָה וְאִישׁ לֹא יְדָעָהּ וַתֵּרֶד הָעַיְנָה
וַתְּמַלֵּא כַדָּהּ וַתָּעַל: יז וַיָּרָץ הָעֶבֶד לִקְרָאתָהּ וַיֹּאמֶר הַגְמִיאִינִי נָא מְעַט-מַיִם מִכַּדֵּךְ: יח וַתֹּאמֶר
שְׁתֵה אֲדֹנִי וַתְּמַהֵר וַתֹּרֶד כַּדָּהּ עַל-יָדָהּ וַתַּשְׁקֵהוּ: יט וַתְּכַל לְהַשְׁקֹתוֹ וַתֹּאמֶר גַּם לִגְמַלֶּיךָ אֶשְׁאָב עַד
אִם-כִּלּוּ לִשְׁתֹּת: כ וַתְּמַהֵר וַתְּעַר כַּדָּהּ אֶל-הַשֹּׁקֶת וַתָּרָץ עוֹד אֶל-הַבְּאֵר לִשְׁאֹב וַתִּשְׁאַב לְכָל-גְּמַלָּיו

**15** And it came to pass, before he had done speaking, that, behold, Rebekah came out, who was born to Bethuel the son of Milcah, the wife of Nahor, Abraham's brother, with her pitcher upon her shoulder. **16** And the damsel was very fair to look upon, a virgin, neither had any man known her; and she went down to the fountain, and filled her pitcher, and came up. **17** And the servant ran to meet her, and said: 'Give me to drink, I pray thee, a little water of thy pitcher.' **18** And she said: 'Drink, my lord'; and she hastened, and let down her pitcher upon her hand, and gave him drink. **19** And when she had done giving him drink, she said: 'I will draw for thy camels also, until they have done drinking.' **20** And she hastened, and emptied her pitcher into the trough, and ran again unto the well to draw, and drew for all his camels.

**- Genesis 24:15-20**

## Questions for Discussion:

1. Chapter 24 of Genesis tells the whole story of how Rebecca becomes Isaac's wife. If you had been in Rebecca's place, would you have made the same decisions?

2. The importance of chesed is found in many of our texts. In Pirkei Avot it is written that the world is founded on three things: Torah, avodah (prayer), and g'milut chasadim (acts of loving-kindness). The rabbis also taught, "In three respects are g'milut chasadim superior to charity: Charity can be done only with one's money, whereas g'milut chasadim can be done with one's person and one's money; charity can be given only to the poor, whereas g'milut chasadim can be done for both the rich and the poor; charity can be given to the living only, whereas g'milut chasadim can be done both for the living and the dead [by attending to funeral needs]." (Tractate Sukkah 49b) How can we show chesed without feeling overwhelmed by the many ways we might be of help? How do we model chesed, both giving and receiving it?

3. Rebecca is known for her kindness, based on her actions in the text above. Chesed (kindness) is, of course, a significant Jewish value and behavior we strive to nurture in the children we teach. We see Rebecca fulfill her responsibility to help take care of the world by providing chesed to another person. What do you think your children will respond when you ask them why they think Rebecca did what she did? What acts of chesed have you done recently? What acts of chesed have others done for you? What acts of kindness have you seen your children do? What would they say if you asked them what acts of chesed they've done recently?

The story of Rebecca is in Parashat Hayyei Sarah.

## Family Reunions

*December 2009*

---

דַ וַיִּשְׁלַח יַעֲקֹב מַלְאָכִים לְפָנָיו אֶל-עֵשָׂו אָחִיו אַרְצָה שֵׂעִיר שְׂדֵה אֱדֹום: ה וַיְצַו אֹתָם
לֵאמֹר כֹּה תֹאמְרוּן לַאדֹנִי לְעֵשָׂו כֹּה אָמַר עַבְדְּךָ יַעֲקֹב עִם-לָבָן גַּרְתִּי וָאֵחַר עַד-עָתָּה:
ו .... וָאֶשְׁלְחָה לְהַגִּיד לַאדֹנִי לִמְצֹא-חֵן בְּעֵינֶיךָ: ז וַיָּשֻׁבוּ הַמַּלְאָכִים אֶל-יַעֲקֹב לֵאמֹר
בָּאנוּ אֶל-אָחִיךָ אֶל-עֵשָׂו וְגַם הֹלֵךְ לִקְרָאתְךָ וְאַרְבַּע-מֵאוֹת אִישׁ עִמּוֹ: ח וַיִּירָא יַעֲקֹב
מְאֹד....

**4** Jacob sent messengers ahead of him to his brother Esau, to Edom's Field in the Seir area. **5** He instructed them to deliver the following message: 'To my lord Esau. Your humble servant Jacob says: I have been staying with Laban, and have delayed my return until now. **6** I ... am now sending word to tell my lord, to gain favor in your eyes.' **7** The messengers returned to Jacob with the report: 'We came to your brother Esau, and he is also heading toward you. He has 400 men with him.' **8** Jacob was very frightened and distressed....

**- Genesis 32:4-8**

---

*Have your Chumash or Tanach (Bible) available to help with this month's shiur!*

**Questions for Discussion:**

1. Share a story of a reunion you've had with someone long lost.

2. The story of Jacob and Esau's reunion, which begins in the text box above, continues in parashat Vayishlach. As a staff, retell the background story of Jacob and Esau, to insure everyone understands why Jacob is "very frightened" in the text above. You can find their story in Genesis 25:19-32 and 27:1-28:9. Jacob's story continues from chapter 28 to Vayishlach, which begins in chapter 32.

   - Once everyone understands Jacob's fear, make some predictions. Will this reunion go well for Jacob? Does he deserve to have it go well? What is the deal with family reunions anyway? Why is it so important (and why is it sometimes so hard) to make it work with family?

   - Predictions in hand, read about the rest of Jacob and Esau's reunion in Genesis 32:9-33:17. Were your predictions correct? If you were already familiar with the story, did you notice anything new when you read it this time? How was this journey of reunion transformative for Jacob?

   - A little later in the Torah, in Parashat Vayiggash, Jacob has another reunion, this time with his son Joseph. You can read about it in Genesis 45:21-46:30. See any similarities? Striking differences? What can we learn from Jacob and his family reunions?

---

3. As we approach Hanukkah and the potential of family gatherings, we can take a lesson from Jacob to teach our children that the Jewish people are one family, and that those things that unite us as a family must be strong enough to overcome the hurts and disagreements that sometimes come along with being a family. The youngest children can use this opportunity to expand their concept of "family" to include extended family members they may not see very often. With older children, talk about the family gatherings that Jacob has in the Torah. What might children find significant about Jacob's reunions? Compare those to the family gatherings the children might have during Hanukkah (or had during Thanksgiving).

## Gratitude

*November 2009*

---

Everything's a dollar,
A dollar twenty-five.
Haven't got a dollar,
But I'm glad to be alive.

An attitude of gratitude,
Hooray for what's okay!
Say thank you with emphatitude
And it's a brand new day.

**- Excerpts from "An Attitude of Gratitude" by Jimmy Buffet, on *Thanks & Giving* by Marlo Thomas and Friends.**

The book and CD *Thanks & Giving*, were created by Marlo Thomas, creator of *Free to Be You and Me*. One hundred percent of the royalties go to St. Jude Children's Research Hospital.

---

**Questions for Discussion:**

1. Share something for which you are thankful with the rest of the staff. Listen as each person shares something for which she is thankful.

2. Do you naturally have an "attitude of gratitude"? Think about people you know who do, and some who don't. Do you think that outlook on life is a matter of nature or nuture?

3. The Hebrew term for gratitude is *hikarat hatov*, which means, literally, "recognizing the good." Practicing gratitude means recognizing the good that is already in your life. Judaism is highly focused on gratitude. We learn from Ben Zoma, "Who is rich? He who rejoices in his lot" *(Pirkei Avot 4:1)*. The tenth commandment often is translated as "you shall not covet," but in her book *The Ten Good Rules*, Susan Remick Topek simply translates, "Be happy with what you have." Think about who, and what, you might be thankful to. The rabbis tell us we should say 100 blessings a day, expressing our gratitude when we wake, wash our hands, wear new clothes, eat a snack. That covers the things for which we are thankful to God, but what about other kinds of things? Do we always express our gratitude to the friend who drove our child home from school? To the car that started when we turned the key? Talk about how we can practice gratitude by making thanks-giving part of our everyday lives.

4. How do you foster an attitude of gratitude in children? How do you anchor this attitude in a Jewish context? What does this look like for toddlers? For four year olds?

Check out this video for a fun look at life without gratitude:
http://www.aish.com/v/49082446.html.

---

## Asking Questions/Parashat Shemot

*January 2006*

> There are few things I respect more than a really good question.
>
> **- Joseph Aaron, editor of the *Chicago Jewish News*, quoted in the *Jewish Advocate*, November 3-9, 1995.**

**Questions for Discussion:**

1. What's so great about a really good question? Why do we always say, "There are no stupid questions"?

2. Are you a questioner? Are you comfortable challenging ideas and seeking more information?

3. Jewish tradition is grounded in questions and discussion. In the Torah, Abraham and others questioned and challenged God. The rabbis of the Talmud questioned and pondered each word of the Torah, seeking meaning and creating interpretations and laws by which we still live today. When we approach text, we ask it questions in order to get to the heart of the mater, the deeper substance. **What questions might you ask of the following text?** (Don't worry about the answers):

   *Exodus 1:15-21. From Parashat Shemot*

   **15** And the king of Egypt spoke to the Hebrew midwives, one of whom was named Shiphrah, and the other Puah; **16** and he said: "When you deliver the Hebrew women, look at the birthstool: if it is a son, kill him; but if it is a daughter, let her live." **17** But the midwives feared God, and did not do as the king of Egypt commanded them, but saved the boys alive. **18** And the king of Egypt called for the midwives, and said to them: "Why have you done this thing, and have saved the boys alive?" **19** And the midwives said to Pharaoh: "Because the Hebrew women are not as the Egyptian women; for they are lively, and are delivered before the midwife can come to them." **20** And God dealt well with the midwives; and the people multiplied, and increased greatly. **21** And it came to pass, because the midwives feared God, that He established households for them.

   After you've come up with some questions, where might you go to find some answers?

4. How can you create a culture that encourages investigation and asking really good questions in your classroom? How do you encourage children to ask questions?

## Shem Tov – A Good Name

*January 2009*

---

מדרש תנחומא פרשת ויקהל סימן א

אַתְּ מוֹצֵא שְׁלֹשָׁה שֵׁמוֹת נִקְרְאוּ לוֹ לְאָדָם. אֶחָד מַה שֶּׁקּוֹרְאִים לוֹ אָבִיו וְאִמּוֹ,
וְאֶחָד מַה שֶּׁקּוֹרְאִין לוֹ בְּנֵי אָדָם, וְאֶחָד מַה שֶּׁקּוֹנֶה הוּא לְעַצְמוֹ. טוֹב מִכֻּלָּן
מַה שֶּׁקּוֹנֶה הוּא לעצמו.

There are three names by which a person is called: one which his parents call him, one which people call him, and one which he earns for himself. The last is the best one of all.

**- Midrash Tanhuma, Parshat VaYakhel 1**

---

**Questions for Discussion:**

1. Why would the name that someone earns for him or herself be the best name?

2. What are your own different names? How did you get these names? Which is your best name?

3. This shiur is loosely inspired by Shemot, the Torah portion we read January 17, 2009: "These are the names (sh'mot) of the children of Israel who came to Egypt with Jacob…". (Exodus 1:1) While the Torah is filled with genealogical lists of names, the rabbis concerned themselves with the value of a good name. In Ecclesiastes (Kohelet) 7:1, we read, "A good name is better than fragrant oil." And "Rabbi Simeon said: There are three crowns. The crown of Torah, the crown of priesthood and the crown of kingship. But the crown of a good name (shem tov) excels them" (Ethics of the Fathers 4:17). What is meant by "a good name"? How do we go about achieving a good name? Is this connected to the best name being the one that a person earns for him or herself?

4. So what does a good name have to do with early childhood? Everything. Having a shem tov means being the very best person you can be. Earning a name for yourself means being a positive part of a community. At the most basic level, a person with a shem tov is someone who plays well with others, who is not afraid to go out and become the person he or she is meant to be. As a teacher, you can give very young children the tools to begin to earn themselves a name, to help them create for themselves a shem tov, a good name with which to take on the world. How will you do this in your classroom?

---

## Talking About God

*February 2009*

---

Rabbi David Wolpe on addressing children's questions about God:

"Our answers to these questions guide our children's view of the universe. What do we wish them to believe - that they are accidents of ancient chemistry or sparks of the divine? Whatever one's philosophy on these matters, we owe our children an honest and searching discussion."

**- From "How to Talk to Your Kids about God" by Rabbi David Wolpe**
http://www.jewishfamily.com/families/features/talk_kids_god.txt

---

**Questions for Discussion:**

1.  What is the scariest thing about talking with children about God?

2.  Who do you turn to, who could you turn to, when children ask challenging questions about God?

3.  Ask yourselves: "What is my connection with God? Do I have a connection with God? What do I wrestle with?" Discuss the answers as a staff.

4.  "Wherever children are learning there dwells a divine presence" (Yiddish proverb). Think about moments in your class when that divine presence has become apparent, moments of wonder, or to quote Rabbi Abraham Joshua Heschel, moments of "radical amazement." Share some of these moments. Then think together about how you mark these moments in the classroom, and as a community take note of the presence of God. With a blessing? With a special song? With a quiet but awe-inspired conversation? How could you be more intentional in marking moments of divine presence, or radical amazement, in your classroom?

5.  When children ask about God, they usually have their own theories. As a staff, role-play conversations with children about God. Generate questions the children might ask, or have asked in the past. Test out using such language as, "Tell me what you think about God." or "I don't know. What do you think? I wonder about that too." or "Some people believe..." "I wonder how God..." "We can thank God for...." Continue to check in as a staff as you venture into the classroom to have these conversations with children.

---

## Kashrut and Holiness

*April 2010*

---

**ויקרא** 11:2-4 פרשת שמיני

זֹאת הַחַיָּה אֲשֶׁר תֹּאכְלוּ מִכָּל-הַבְּהֵמָה אֲשֶׁר עַל-הָאָרֶץ : כֹּל מַפְרֶסֶת פַּרְסָה וְשֹׁסַעַת שֶׁסַע פְּרָסֹת מַעֲלַת גֵּרָה בַּבְּהֵמָה אֹתָהּ תֹּאכֵלוּ : אַךְ אֶת-זֶה לֹא תֹאכְלוּ מִמַּעֲלֵי הַגֵּרָה וּמִמַּפְרִסֵי הַפַּרְסָה אֶת-הַגָּמָל כִּי-מַעֲלֵה גֵרָה הוּא וּפַרְסָה אֵינֶנּוּ מַפְרִיס טָמֵא הוּא לָכֶם :

**ויקרא** 20:25-26פרשת קדושים

וְהִבְדַּלְתֶּם בֵּין-הַבְּהֵמָה הַטְּהֹרָה לַטְּמֵאָה וּבֵין-הָעוֹף הַטָּמֵא לַטָּהֹר .... וִהְיִיתֶם לִי קְדֹשִׁים כִּי קָדוֹשׁ אֲנִי ה'....

These are the creatures that you may eat from among all the land animals: any animal that has true hoofs, with clefts through the hoofs, and that chews the cud – such you may eat. The following, however, of those that either chew the cud or have true hoofs, you shall not eat: the camel – although it chews the cud, it has no true hoofs: it is unclean for you.

**- Leviticus 11:2-4 Shemini**

So shall you set apart the clean beast from the unclean, the unclean bird from the clean.... You shall be holy to Me, for I the Lord am holy....

**- Leviticus 20:25-26 (excerpts) Kedoshim**

---

**Questions for Discussion:**

1. This year, in April we read in the Torah about which animals, fish, and insects are permitted for the Jewish people to eat; in other words, what is kosher. As a staff, share what you know about keeping kosher: the laws, the challenges, where to get the best kosher Chinese food.

2. If you keep kosher, think about your "kashrut story." Have you kept kosher since you were a kid? Did you take on this mitzvah as an adult? Have you changed the way you keep kosher over the years? What have your challenges been? Your greatest satisfactions with keeping kosher? If you first encountered kashrut when you became a teacher at this school, what has been most interesting to you? Most challenging?

3. The Torah and later the rabbis clearly view keeping kosher as a way to infuse our daily lives with holiness. In today's world, the holiness of eating can be understood in so many ways. What we eat affects our carbon footprint, so we make decisions about buying locally grown or organic foods. What we eat affects the lives of others, so we make decisions based on how the workers or animals are treated, using guides such as Magen Tzedek (http://magentzedek.org/), Fair Trade (http://www.wfto.com/) or Tav

---

HaYosher (http://tavhayosher.wordpress.com/). How do these considerations affect the holiness of the act of eating? How might keeping kosher affect our level of holiness? How does kashrut intersect with all these other considerations? (Be sure to have some fair trade, kosher, 72 percent cocoa dark chocolate bars on hand for this discussion!)

4. There is some basic information about keeping kosher in a Conservative early childhood program in the *Vision for Conservative Early Childhood Programs* (pp. 94-95) (http://uscj.org/images/ECE_vision.pdf). How do we use kashrut, and the blessings we say at snack and lunch time, to infuse children with a sense of holiness?

## Kibbud Av V'em/Mother's Day

*May 2009*

> Brian woke up feeling great! He ran into the kitchen, and gave his mother a kiss and a great big hug. "I love you, Mom! You're the best mom in the whole world!" Brian's mother felt loved and appreciated. Because Brian's mom was feeling loved and appreciated, she made Brian and his sister, Joanna, their favorite breakfast....
>
> **- From *Because Brian Hugged His Mother* by David Rice, Dawn Publications, 1999**

**Questions for Discussion:**

1. Mother's Day is coming. Talk about ways you have shown *kavod*, respect, toward your mom, or have been shown kavod, if you are a mom. Did this show of kavod ever lead to a whole chain of positive events, as it does in *Because Brian Hugged His Mother*?

2. The fifth commandment is *kibbud av v'em*, honor your father and mother. What does this mean? How do we honor someone? Is honoring the same as loving?

3. A story about kibbud av v'em appears in the *Vision for Conservative Early Childhood Programs* (page 18). It begins, "One summer morning, Dima ben Netina was working in his jewelry store. As he worked he whistled happily but very softly, because he did not want to wake his father, who had fallen fast asleep on a large chest-like box in a corner of the store." (Read the entire story at http://uscj.org/images/ECE_vision.pdf) Stories like this one, as well as secular stories like *Because Brian Hugged His Mother* and *A Chair for My Mother* by Vera Williams (Greenwillow Books, 1982), can help young children become well versed at the very Jewish concept of honoring our parents. What other sources do you know of that teach this mitzvah?

4. As you are decorating picture frames or planting flowers to send home as gifts for Mother's Day, how can you also address the bigger idea (some would say the enduring understanding, or what we really want children to remember forever) of Mother's Day being about relationships, and the ideal way to treat our parents all year round? How can you help the children you teach think about how they can be respectful and/or helpful to their parents?

CPSIA information can be obtained at www.ICGtesting.com
Printed in the USA
BVOW06s1430090714

357952BV00010B/49/P